DREAMALITY

FREEDUMB
OR
FREEDOM

SHAWN BOSI

Gotham Books

30 N Gould St.
Ste. 20820, Sheridan, WY 82801
https://gothambooksinc.com/

Phone: 1 (307) 464-7800

© 2024 *Shawn Bosi*. All rights reserved.

No part of this book may be reproduced, stored in a retrieval system, or transmitted by any means without the written permission of the author.

Published by Gotham Books (January 17, 2024)

ISBN: 979-8-88775-231-0 (H)
ISBN: 979-8-88775-519-9 (P)
ISBN: 979-8-88775-230-3 (E)

Because of the dynamic nature of the Internet, any web addresses or links contained in this book may have changed since publication and may no longer be valid.

The views expressed in this work are solely those of the author and do not necessarily reflect the views of the publisher, and the publisher hereby disclaims any responsibility for them.

TABLE OF CONTENTS

INTRODUCTION I

CHAPTERS

IT'S A SIGN! 1

FASTER THAN A SPEEDING BULLET! 4

MY GAL CAL 7

A DREAM 18

DREAMS BEFORE WORK 24

DELIVER US LORD FROM EVERY EVIL 31

GOD'S FURRIERY 37

"CONFRONTED BY SCRIPTURE" 42

LIFE OF MIRRORS 45

DREAMING WITH AN ANGEL 53

BELIEVING IS SEEING 70

THE SLOW ECONOMY 79

RAVEN 95

PAY ATTENTION TO DETAILS 125

THE HAWAII WINTER GATEWAY (S) 136

THE MISSILE ALERT 167

DA LION'S DEN 176

DEUCES WILD 187

INTRODUCTION

The mail came today, mostly junk mail. Junk mail has taken on a whole new form within my life. I have been including my bills in the junk mail category; actually, much of everything that arrived.

Why is today different? Today I felt the need to open the mail right away. I noticed a letter from Hawaii, it surprised me. I immediately began to think to myself,

"Seldom do I receive good mail for my company!
It's named, "Upright Fences Downright Patios".
The Operation Manager usually handles the bulk.

I opened the letter with excitement. My spirit sensed a special importance was sealed within. My hands couldn't open it fast enough. A business card fell out twirling towards the floor. The color purple caught my attention as it floated downwards.

My body became frozen in the moment as I tried to catch it. The refractions of light seemed to be hitting thousands of crystals along the highlighted path to my feet. I froze within my own steps. A rock within ice was my state. The letter swooped to the floor. The name Katz was written as a return address.

The name didn't ring a bell to me. It wasn't really clear in my mind. Who is this? Why would they be writing? What was the significance within this letter? Hawaii! I met this woman at the writer's conference. What could she want with me?

She wrote "Dear Shawn, you made the local news!" I spotted a news article in the envelope. "It's a Sign! Aloha! Katz "was written across it with a marker.

How could she have known? I had experienced a sign? Was she just referring to this paper article in Maui?

The answer to that question is now! I was slightly confused but perplexed. I live in the moment! Yes! It is a sign! Yes! It has meaning! It especially had meaning to me in the here and now! Spirit interpreted messages. What meaning do they hold?

I walked towards the bathroom and noticed a strange haze at the door. What is this strange mist within the room? This has never happened here!

The ceilings are large and open. I should know; I was the designer! This couldn't be happening!

My body began to seize. I could hardly keep my grip on the book I was prepared to read, nonetheless myself! I stumbled towards the Jacuzzi and stepped in. The warm water covered my body. Strange words were in my mind. They seemed to be in Japanese and American languages.

The thoughts that filled my mind were:

1) If you are not in control, it doesn't mean you're out of control. Control is within your hands and your mind.

2) Your intellect is first within your heart. Then second within the mind. Do not allow it to interfere with your heart's desires. What you have to do is say, Yes! There is no need to worry about how. Or even when! How is up to you or better worded, Me!

3) Just believe deeply; within your heart all things are possible.

4) They are plans for your life. These plans are in detail, and you should know. In other words, I am . . .

I could not delineate any more of the message due to the unfamiliar language. The continuous repeating in the background sounded over and over. They sounded like an orchestra within the arena of my mind. Things began to slur and the words continued.

What is the meaning of all of this? What is the special message I'm not receiving? These were the questions I had. As I regained consciousness all the thoughts were interwoven. Was it some type of divine chemistry? A blob of notes all related to one another. Was there more to the last message? Or did it simply end stating, I am?

I began to search my mind. I tried to remember how the words fit together. I considered opening my eyes. My fingertips followed as the rest of my body stopped shaking.

"Do you know, these plans for your life are detailed? I am!" The voice shattered the room and echoed off the water which was cooling.

The book was riding a wave. Performing like a professional surfer on Hana preparing to be a star. Goosebumps engulfed my body as my mind disappeared into the peaceful silence… I opened my eyes, and the haze was still there. Then I noticed the writing across the mirror. Someone wrote, "It's a sign!"

CHAPTER I

IT'S A SIGN!

The words across the mirror were written in the English language. I thought it could be considered weird. It was much deeper than that. It was a sign that spirits do exist! The spirit that appeared wasn't just from my mind, it was real! It can be intermediated as a Divine Intervention!

I said to myself, "how am I to interpret this?" Who is behind this mysterious message? Does this have anything to do with the Gala Event the other night? Was it from Amber, my dog? Amber was a Pit Bull that had passed about four years ago.

In some religions it is said that the animal contains a human spirit. Do you believe this? Many cultures fear the spirit of animals especially if you had mistreated them. How will they retaliate in the spirit? What a mystery!

I must relax! The presence of whatever it was fills the room. I am not surprised the white haze has now encompassed most of the bedroom as well. It seems as if someone is pouring cold water on coals somewhere inside of the house. Only Steven Schussler has ever lived with a haze in his house quite like this and it came from fog machines. This is quite different yet similar to The Rain Forest Café.

I rose from the tub and felt the heated tile beneath my feet. It was like walking over wet sand on a hot day. My feet began to slide but I maintained my balance.

I looked back at the tub and noticed both the letter and the book sinking further into the water. They were totally soaked as I retrieved what was left of the smeared ink and wet paper they were written on.

Was it the letter that brought the strange mist to the room? I wasn't ready to decipher it at the time. I needed to towel off and get in some shorts. I was looking forward to a relaxing moment in front of the fireplace.

As I sat in front of the fireplace, I noticed the presence of the strange spirit that still filled the room. Why is it still present? What can this be?

It felt like a protective shield surrounding me. Was it protecting me? Was some dangerous thing about to happen?

I began to have a conversation with it. "How and why do I feel you are protecting me? I know you are still here! Can you hear me?"

Within a few seconds the floor gave a shutter. I knew it was an answer. The radio became filled with static. Then I heard the words, "I know you didn't bring me out here to drown!" My eyes began to swell with tears and my emotions have left the framework of my body they were just in.

Was it possible, my deceased dog's voice was coming through the airways? Or was it some other person from my past trying to contact me?

The words registered deeply within my soul because the last moments of Amber's life were spent in my arms outside in my swimming pool. I had carried her outside awaiting the veterinarian's arrival. My parents pleaded with me not to hold her underwater. I simply wanted her body to stop seizing. I knew she was stubborn like her owner and did not want to let go. I had made the decision to take her out of the misery she had been experiencing the last three days.

What exactly did the spiritual guide mean three days ago- when she mentioned an "Amber Alert for Halloween Night"? Halloween is nearly three days away and why exactly did I have to get the mail myself today anyway?

The thought of Jesus rising in three days gave me comfort that it might be Amber. No! It couldn't be! I knew in my heart that she was leading me to something greater! It was a sign.

I find myself constructing the correct words which escape from my mind. . . I had a touch of a struggle with that but the mist mysteriously disappeared. I took a deep breath and my mind separated from the crazy thoughts.

Once you have experienced something like this, it takes more than a moment to interpret it. Very clearly the intentions sink away, and you think about what is behind it all. The thought of reality hits and you try to make sense out of the situation. Was it as I call it, Dreamality?"

CHAPTER II

FASTER THAN A SPEEDING BULLET!

The best escape from this situation was to leave my home and take a drive. I knew the thoughts in my mind were confusing but real. I wasn't going to allow them to confuse me any further.

A cruise down the highway sometimes helps. I find it a touch relaxing!

I quickly dressed, knowing my gray colored Mustang was waiting for me in the garage. It would do the trick. I find it at times, faster than a speeding bullet. I couldn't escape the room fast enough. I entered the garage and saw my little piece of happiness. My silver Mustang! The legendary growl of the engine cleared my mind of the confusion I had faced. I inserted the key into the ignition and turned it. The sound of the engine thrilled me with great excitement! The shine that appeared across the hood excited my intentions. Peace overcame my mind as I slipped her into reverse.

What a silver beauty, and so much speed! I couldn't wait to get her on the back roads to open her up. Full acceleration was my thought! Why not! If it has it, use it!

I headed towards the open highway called Interstate 355. Looking up towards the sky I noticed the cloud formations. They had the shapes of horseshoes, but others reminded me of beautiful Angels.

The thought reminded me of my personal angel and best friend, Cal. Cal is my girlfriend. She is a very special Angel to me. I knew it was another sign. This is going to be a great day. As the hum of my engine continued, the speedometer began to give a signal of high speed. This pony gives the pony another meaning. As I drove down the ramp a black monster appeared behind me. It was a newer model GTO. I had no fear as the two-ton black beauty was approaching my backside. Just knowing what my stallion could do, I laughed! Once down the ramp and on the highway, I gunned it. I quickly left the black predator behind me.

It wasn't too long before I saw it approaching me. The GTO and its passenger sped past me at a high speed. I thought to myself, "Let me give this guy a run for his money!" I accelerated even harder as I watched the numbers on the dash disappear. "What an exciting run this will be,' I thought to myself…

Suddenly I heard a voice from above shout, "Slowdown!" all the confusion from home had followed me. The same voice that saved me from drowning is now controlling my automobile. Who can this be? I slowed the car down and the GTO sped by.

I knew in my mind I would have blown that black beauty into the dust. I was interrupted by this unusual spirit. It seems to be controlling the things I do. In a way, I like it but when it comes to my fun time, no way!

Once again, I began thinking. The only thought that seemed to fit the situation was "God's Pace!" That's it! I must learn to do things at the pace set by the Lord. This was the intervention of God's Angels. Slowing me down was deliberate. Its intentions were intended strictly for me. Yes, me! The driver of this silver bullet! This is how God's Pace came to be. It came directly for me, the driver!

I am a true Christian, and the Lord will protect. I feel he has sent an Angel to watch over me. If that's the case, I do feel well protected. The Bible states Angels watch over people. I guess I have a few watching me when I'm on the move! All the things I do! I don't feel it's wrong, but let a man have some fun.

I turned the gray stallion around and headed to Cal's house. I wouldn't have any problems while enjoying her company. I call her Cal only because she mentions how much she loves the State. Her favorite song is," Going back to Cali," by LL Cool Jay!

CHAPTER III

MY GAL CAL

My gal Cal is a beautiful, full spirited woman. She is kind and always loves me with great intentions. She is twenty-six years of age.

When I first met her, she spoke of her past relationships. She stated to me that her last love was involved with some shady characters. I was told that this person was still watching her at her apartment. An apartment he paid for her to live in.

I remember laughing and taking another swallow of my drink. I looked her in the eyes and said, "so what! Some of my family members are connected. I didn't go into specifics but tried to calm her. I guess it worked. She picked up her glass and began to finish the drink in front of her. She ended the conversation with, "yes," but is he Mafia? I ignored the question.

Cal explained how frightened she was of him. She explained how he pushed her through the glass shower doors in the bathroom. She was left bleeding and didn't speak for days. I concluded she doesn't have much luck with men. She was in another relationship when she found her boyfriend hanging. She explained how she attempted to cut the thick rope that suspends him. She used manicuring scissors. I was surprised how she spoke of her past and how hard life was.

I cleared my thoughts and prepared myself to see her. I was just around the corner from her house when another thought crossed my mind. I asked myself if I should tell her about the strange haze in the bathroom. She probably would ask me if I smoked a joint. I know that would be the first statement from her mouth. I think a ride to my home would be better. I would take her into the room and show her the haze if it's still there. It probably won't be but that's to be determined. If it isn't there, I will recreate the scene and see if it reappears while I'm in her company. Just a crazy thought and it even surprises me that it crossed my mind.

I pulled into the drive and gave the engine a good push with the accelerator. A real attention getter! I guess it worked. Cal suddenly appeared at the window. She waved me in as I cut the engine. I exited from the car and confronted her at the door. "Ready for a ride," I asked. I couldn't help notice her beauty. She had a green scarf around her soft neck.

I guess she knew I would be stopping by. She was ready to ride, and I was just as eager. I always notice how well she is dressed… I asked her to turn around so I could look at her beauty.

She swung around but seemed to freeze during the motion. She grabbed my hand and pulled my body towards the machine waiting in the drive. I didn't have too much time to enjoy her beauty, but I was pleased to be in her company. Cal is a real beauty, and her company relaxes me in a way.

I opened the door as a gentleman would do for a real woman. Most women have understood when the polite gesture has stopped in my past. I do not foresee stopping anytime soon when it comes to Cali. She entered and sat down with a great smile across her face. I smiled back and shut the door. As I walked around the silver Mustang a glitter came from her clean hair through the rear window. It made her smile. I sat in the driver's seat and looked over towards her, noticing her beauty yet again.

I was proud that she was in my company and my ride. What a match! A beautiful woman sitting in a stud's Mustang. Had to say stud there, no pun intended. Get ready for a ride of your life Cal! She turned towards me and smiled. She states with excitement, "Yes!"

I tapped the key and heard the engine start to roar. The excitement of the sound thrilled her. I knew she loved it by the look across her face. Pretty ladies love pretty things, especially when they are just as great looking.

She relaxed into the padding of the leather seat, ready for the ride. I popped the transmission into gear and down the drive we rolled. Her and I; "What a pair," I thought. I headed towards Maple Lake. A secluded fall wonderland placed carefully by God in the woods. I could enjoy Cal and yet share the excitement of the scenery. What a coloring book! The blues of the water seemed to sparkle. The air contained a fresh smell of mountain marrow. The sun hit the windshield as we passed the lake. Cal enjoys the scenery and the ride through the woods.

Neither one of us has said a word in the last fifteen minutes. God's presentation isn't complete until a Fox appears to the right of the road.

Cali's thoughts are beautiful; I am hearing them clearly now. She looks at me and smiles. She hers mine as well.

I hold her hand as she hears my mind say the words "we are so connected." "We are almost one!" She squeezes my hand in return.

No words are spoken but my hand is being held by an enlightened hand. These exchanges of simple phrases become quite easy once we connect further with one another. Especially after long nature hikes in the forest or the "woods" as Cali would call them.

I had enough of the ride, and it was time to get back to the haze. The thought wouldn't escape my mind. I must tell her! I turned the car around and headed towards my house. I was determined to tell her. How?

How would she conclude this sight? It took my breath away. The thought of rejection or even her thinking I am out of my mind. What will she conclude at the end?

I sped through the woods and made it to the highway. I followed the road towards my house. It wined and turned yet was a distance from the woods. I pulled into the drive and asked Cal to accompany me in the house.

She was happy to follow me up the walk and into the front room. She made some slight sighs of approval as her eyes traced the curve of my butt in my jeans. I just couldn't tell her of the event, so I devised a plan to get into the hot tub. I knew she wouldn't object. I went into the room and began to fill it. Cal was fixing the cocktails as the tub filled.

Through the door appeared Cal. She placed her drink at the corner of the tub. She began to look around trying hard to speak. Her body began to shake and her hand trembled handing me my drink. The haze fills the room. She was not in the same space as me but was concerned about the haze. I like to be referred to as a spirit. The spirit seemed to spend 70% of the time with me and where else, I just didn't know.

Cali began to get nervous. Her toes began tapping lightly against the heated tile floor.

She asked, "How can you remain so calm? Aren't you nervous about the situation we're in? "

The realization had begun to set in. I was in this with her now and had no idea how quickly we arrived where we are today.

Shawn! I have an idea! Will you run away with me, and we could work this out? Sell the business, or just leave it!

I started my business in November of 1998. I was working with an editor to get my first book out on the market. I never thought she would ask me to sell my business; yet to leave, with her, for some unknown place. To run away was just not an option. I wouldn't do it. I learned many lessons. Running away wasn't an option. Life is not the breath you take. You need to stay and win the race. Don't let life take your breath away for any reason. You need to face your fears and they will disappear. You just might miss the point but stick it out! Shawn! "I know you're determined but am I worth it to you?"

I looked deeply into her eyes. I replied, "Dunkin Donuts Style!" Our eyes met and didn't part for minutes. I was sure she knew I would give her what she needed to hear. I answered, "Yes!"

I could not believe the words I heard spoken from my mouth. Why did she steal my heart like this? Why did I permit this to happen to me?

The conversations lead deeply into the night. We passed the front door to get to my room. I noticed the door was open and unlocked. I know we locked it before going upstairs. Suddenly a flash of light came across the windows. "What was that strange light," I asked?

Cali couldn't explain it. The things that were happening we were not able to explain. "Don't worry Cal! Let's get some sleep." I am brought face to face with the computer screen upstairs and I see the title "Deuces Wild". I stare at the clock, and it is 2:22!

Cali awakes while pressing her already moistened lips on my mouth . She is reaching and stretching to turn off an alarm as it flashes 2:22, her scent more vibrant and seductive than usual!

"I like it so far" Cali ads. I can't imagine waking any better than this! I can't believe it is only 2:22! Cali says, "make a wish!" And the s becomes a z and pretty soon the z becomes an s. "Swishhh! Swishhh! Swissssh!"

Suddenly her phone rang, and a voice began to speak as she answered it. I pretended to be asleep; as if somehow this made our situation safer to be in. She didn't mention to the person on the other end of the line that I was right next to her in the bed. I figured if she did it could be fatal. I did not move.

Shawn, Why are you holding what's left of that necklace in your hand? Believe me; when the necklace shattered off her neck, Cali began to understand why I was as spiritual as I was. The necklace her California friend, Pan, had made for her; was a blown glass piece shaped like a teardrop with glistening colors. She was discussing the government secret her deceased boyfriend had shared with her prior to hanging himself.

The death of her boyfriend when it occurred was tragic! His life was taken by himself: Cali smokes a cigarette outside while she thinks about how much he has been drinking.

She begins to realize everything he is going through is just way too much. "It is the government who insists the information does not get out there!" Cali's boyfriend begins to shout.

He had discovered a secret that would change America! He was not supposed to share it with anyone.

He just shared the secret with Cali, his soulmate. The government is coming after him anyway and he needed to share it with somebody. He begs her not to mention it to anyone else. He is scared for his and her safety.

Cali describes returning into the room only to see her drunk boyfriend suspended from the ceiling with a rope.

Cali does everything her one-hundred-pound frame body will allow. She tries to cut down her cousin's hanging body. She "somehow managed to use the sharper portion of manicure scissors to cut the rope – This!"

I remember her saying "This" quite often as I am sure it was a difficult thing to do based upon how she positioned her body while telling the story.

"This! I tell ya! Try to do . . . this; while attempting to save the person that you love!"

I saw her body all curled up. Uncomfortable, with heavy expressions weighing on her face. . . "Thissss!

And the s becomes a z and pretty soon the z becomes a s. "Swishhh! Swishhh! Swissssh!" "Swishhh!", "Swishhh!", "Swissssh!"

The sound was brilliant, and it became loudest right before the necklace blew away from her chest.

It literally lifted 3-4 inches off of her chest. It paused just long enough for both of us to stare at it and one another. Our eyes widened as they met, and our mouths opened; then it shattered off of her neck.

"We need to talk Cali! I really need to talk to you. Sit up!" "Yes", she replied.

Okay! I am not sure why God brought you to me! I am not sure why I felt it was needed for us to attend The Gala Event? I wanted you to go, especially after all the things you have experienced in your lifetime. I did not know Amber was going to appear as she did. A spirit! I am sure it is her!

I tried with all my thoughts to reason with her. Try to make her understand what I was experiencing. She had the ability to listen, but did she understand? Heatherism is what I call it. It is a combination of Heaven and feathers.

I loved the way the words coming from her beautiful lips sounded. "Shawn, we do need to talk about this." Those same words I remember in the past years from my Mother, principal, and others. In this case I knew it contained a different meaning.

She stared into my eyes as hers filled with tears. I love you! I love you! If it's important we should talk.

I shared the details with her of my experience in the tub: the seizures, the signs, and the white midst in the air. I told her the cloud-like presence that filled the room has been with me for a while now. The same presence she witnessed left the room as soon as she mentioned Mr. Mafia's name.

I feel safe when the presence is around me and right now, I don't feel that security. It's gone and I do not feel very comfortable or safe at this moment in time.

I began to pray. Cali was surprised to see the spirit appear once more. You can see it! Can you Cali?

It might have something to do with the book I am writing. I must continue to write! I believe these experiences are occurring because of my thoughts and the body of the text.

"Our spirits act like a key Cali. At least that's the best way I can try to explain understanding and following your spirit. The key feathers itself in and depending upon what set of feelers line up; the key may or may not work to open the door. These spirits are guiding me because I have asked them to guide me, but their messages are sometimes not always clear.

Sometimes, even when they are clear- I do not listen to them and that sets the feelers searching in a whole new direction until they line up again! Not listening to their directions and guidance seems to set them in a frenzy or panic mode!

I have to stress that point. Not listening to our gut sets our feelers searching in a whole new direction. When we elect not to listen to our spirits higher message it begins to desensitize ourselves. Our internal feelers begin a new search within the molecular structure of our bodies traveling through water.

Most of us adults tend not to listen to the messages, sometimes like me on purpose, because sometimes it is something just trying to hold me back. Or someone. Or many; Like a Cabal.

Something does not want me to succeed! I will not subject myself to opening up to them. That is how they get in. For God hath not given us the spirit of fear, but of power, and of love, and of a sound mind. (2 Timothy 1:7)

We need to continue this relationship no matter how scary this becomes. Ok? I feel the light guides me as you do."

Cali smiled and said, "I love you! Shawn! Shawn!" She had a tremendous way of telling me she loved me. She repeats my name a few times and I know the meaning.

Cali. Cali! Just relax. Do not allow him to steal your energy. He needs it to survive and fuel his negative behaviors. Consider him to be a vampire from now on." Shawn states all knowingly and guided.

"Believe me, for years I allowed other people to steal energy from me. It is yours and it is precious. Breathe and relax. "

It was three days until Halloween, so the vampire comment was appropriate. I looked over to the mirror and again saw the haze. It entered my head and disappeared. What does all this mean?

It appears people who do not fear God have a greater ability to walk through this life with no conscious.

I am confused why lowering standards can sometimes catapult a career. I am determined to live righteously more and more everyday. Everything is a sign or at least a temporary post-it note if it can be heard; then it can be written.

CHAPTER IV

A DREAM

The night passed and I found myself asleep in Cali's arms. What a comforting feeling lying with her. My love for her was real but thinking of selling the business wasn't an option nor would I run.

My mind was in turmoil. I tried to ease it, but nothing I did seemed to work. I cleared my head of all the Mafia talk. This seemed to work best. It was the first time that evening I felt at ease. My thoughts were on nothing and anything. All I wanted to do was take each breath until the morning broke.

I lay comfortably in her arms and the dreams began. My mind brought me back to a place long ago. I was in Orlando Florida on New Year's Evening. I was sitting in a pub enjoying a drink. I noticed the beauty of a young lady. She was dancing with a handsome somebody. I thought, "he is a lucky man to know her". She was a beautiful blonde. She had long legs and a face put together like Penelope Cruz in "Elegy". Her look was to die for. There isn't a man in the pub that hadn't drooled over her.

I continued to stare at the beautiful couple as my curiosity overcame me. I wondered what they were all about. I couldn't help but notice the lady was trying to make conversation with other men. She did this while dancing in the arms of her lover.

I looked around to see if a single gal was hanging around. I spotted a red headed beauty sitting at the bar. I thought if I asked her to dance; it would give me the opportunity to approach the blonde woman. I felt the need to hold her as he was. It overcame me. I couldn't control the voice inside me demanding her attention. What are they about? I knew in my mind they were strange. I had to do something to introduce myself.

I approached the young woman sitting at the bar. I asked her if she just fell out of Heaven, due to her beauty. The question floored her. She was pleased with smiles. I was just as happy it worked. I use this line often to attract beautiful women. It hasn't failed me yet. The look you get, from blondes to brunettes is great. The eye response is even greater. It helps you score at closing time. This is a great approach. If you think I'm being serious here please move on.

My dream took me further away from the arm safety of Cali. My mind kept the image of the dream gal. I was in the haze in my mind. The mist has taken me far away to an unknown place in Orlando. I let the dream flow as a waterfall in the beauty of a forest. I followed every motive of intention the haze presented. My thoughts were being controlled as my day was in the hot tub.

Dreamality had taken over; bringing me to this place I was a stranger too. I wasn't scared, for I knew I was in the arms of a real beauty, holding me. I knew I was comfortable and safe! I let the haze consume me.

The red head I approached had no name. I couldn't make out what she was saying. My mind was fixated on the blonde, I guess. I can't explain what was going on because the haze was in charge. I had no control as I swept into a cesspool of sex and lust.

It seemed all the people in the pub became swingers. The couple approached me in this dream and tried to convince me to leave with them.

This was my goal and I denied them of the moment. I couldn't figure out why I said no to all their advances and talk to convince me. She said, "he just wanted to watch." It was something my mind wanted but my heart controlled over the situation. It was another sign that I was not to cheat on Cali!

It was a pure indication to me that the Lord has started to clean my heart from the filth of the world. Staying grounded in his word is often not as easy as it is written or said. I don't want to drown! I don't want to drown! I was shouting in my sleep. It woke me and released me from my thoughts of negative persuasion. The members of his donkey-like figure are trying to seduce me!

Shawn! Shawn! You're safe! I am here holding you! Open your eyes and take a deep breath. You were just dreaming. I saw that thing enter the top of your head too. What has it done to you?

I couldn't tell if I dreamed the sign or if the two of them had merged! I struggled to laugh and wanted so much to tell her of the dream. She was partially right and uninformed of where I had been. What I experienced in the pub. I don't want to chase other women in my dreams. I know it was late and talk is cheap. I just asked the Lord to save me as he did and remain the man he made me to be.

The experience had taken much energy from me, and I was past the Orlando state now!

I was floating, feeling like a battery recharging. Sleep! I couldn't tell if it was a dream or reality at the time. Sleep is the best body recharge. This was a time to eliminate as much toxicity in my life as possible. This is not only in my life but through my whole body. Honor the need for solitude and respect your relationship with others; just as I was taught growing up.

My direction was very clear. My director was God. All I have to do is listen and learn from what he said. These are my dreams, my thoughts! This is my space in the book of life he wrote for me!

We as his people just happen to breathe and walk as he did. He is and was, he did, and he does. He died for us! My space in the world is a big portion of this spinning wheel. It is turning our country and I am so proud I was taught to love respectfully! I believe my experiences as a spiritually taught man need to be shared. It is after all, God's Pace!

This slow economy will greatly benefit those who are spiritually grounded and less materialistic. Ironically, the weight of the Egyptian army wagons could have led to their demise. I picture the Lord causing a strong East wind all that night. The waters were a wall to them on their left and right sides. The underwater land bridge at Nuweiba, Egypt created an 8-mile passage to Saudi Arabia. The sea's floor became dry land but only to some extent. The heavy Egyptian army wagons became embedded in the sea's floor as the level rose overnight.

I could have sworn I heard Cali speaking to me, was it now or was it a couple hours ago. Am I even awake? I can not tell but I am up. I see a note left; right below the mirror where the letter was left the night before. Immediately, I see it as a sign for this day. I am struggling to move quickly so I do not think it is a dream anymore. Normally I can move much faster in my dreams, but I am truly struggling. I am drained.

Last night was what I call a spiritual orgasm and they are more intense than a physical one. I can hardly move. I immediately begin to drink water as fast as I humanly can, and my body appears to be glistening from the sparkles of Cali's make-up. The note resting on the mirror is glistening more than anywhere else. "Angel Dust" my mom would call it.

I begin to read what it says and notice the expensive paper it is written on. "I can't believe Cali carries this paper with her in her car! "; was the first thing I think but I begin to read the letter dated October 30'th 2008:

Dear Shawn,

The long night of nurturing sleep has brought the crisp dawn to us along with a refreshed spirit, sense of clarity, and of course a renewal of faith in God (after experiencing that white steam-like image entering into your head) faith is important. The intrinsic beauty of the cyclical nature of life is that every morning, we are patiently provided with a fresh clean slate. If you agree, then, after analysis and renewed faith: I have this to convey to you: The Shawn I like is precisely the Shawn you are in all moments. I respect you for who you are encompassing all faith, owning a business or in relations with or without assets. I especially am thankful for you going through this crazed situation in my life especially with the luck of my last three boyfriends. You are safe Shawn. You are not going to drown. We will be okay. Xoxoxo

CALI

Immediately I began to laugh because she still thinks I thought I was going to drown in the bathtub.

I set everything aside and devoted myself to what matters most. I took baby steps towards my life dreams. I act on gut instincts at times to do what feels right. I met an author at a fueling station near my office; he inspired me to get moving on this story. He promised it would be written with God's time frame. All things in my life must be. He blessed me. I took his number for advice as I could use it. I could not believe I had just met John Sylvester.

The interconnectedness of the meeting with the author at the fueling station and my life was very powerful. My favorite book is "The Way of the Peaceful Warrior" by Dan

Millman. The premise of the story is created as a gymnast attending Berkeley University meets an enlightened man at a fueling station. He named this character Socrates.

The name of the author I met at the fueling station is John Sylvester. My biggest role model growing up was Sylvester Stallone also known as John Rambo. I couldn't have created a more meaningful name or meeting place. I knew I was being guided intrinsically.

When I was compelled to write, I did. I am inspired by it, and I love to tell you about the walk I experience in life.

I have realized that as long as I am experiencing life, writing it down embedded it into memory. My time capsule of life from the past; time our maker gave me within a space of life.

CHAPTER V

DREAMS BEFORE WORK

A day went by since I was with Cal. I relaxed pretty much over the weekend. I was exhausted from the entertainment from the previous evening. I didn't plan anything this week with her. I needed to concentrate on the business.

I woke early because of a restless night. The rain wouldn't quit, and it disturbed my sleep. The clock said 8:00 A.M. and that meant it was time for my workday to begin.

It had been some time since I had a climax. I decided to masturbate before starting my day. It was quite invigorating and that's what I call, "Dreamality!" I enjoyed the time spent and the great relaxation it created. It started my day and I felt wonderful afterwards. A few moments in the shower added to the finish.

After dressing I went into the office to rehearse my schedule for the day. It was quite a busy one but a good one to face. I had two closings scheduled today. The first one was in Palos Heights at 10:30.

I quickly swallowed a cup of coffee and walked over to the answering machine. I reviewed my appointments and listened to my messages. Shawn! This is Bill! I hate to start your morning off with a gripe and bad news but . . . I am calling to tell you that the sign your crew screwed into my new fence has been removed. Your pricing is great but that doesn't mean I would include free advertising for Upright Fences! I took it off. I am a little disturbed now, for I have four holes in my brand-new vinyl fence,

What can be done about this?

Call me!

I need to discuss this with you. I am not too upset because I know you will make it right. You know my number at the office. I will arrive at 10:00 A.M. I will await your call! Don't Forget about me.

I didn't believe the message I heard. This guy thinks I would forget him?

I continued to listen to the next message and plan my day. Shawn, this is Tim. You are doing a job for me down the street from your house. The fence posts are off my property. They need to be moved 10 to 12 inches. According to my plat of survey the posts have been set on my neighbors' property. I guess your crew made a mistake when they reviewed my property line. Give me a call as soon as you get this message. Don't let them proceed until we talk and go over this matter.

Shawn! Give me a call. This is Amanda, your neighbor down the street. The fence posts your crew installed yesterday are in the wrong place and need to be moved. I don't know if Tim got in touch with you so I figured I would leave you a message. If you can't get through to his phone, call my cell. I will be at the beauty shop this afternoon, but I will answer my cell.

Please call one of us as soon as possible. They are on my neighbors' property!

While my salmon was cooking for breakfast I decided to go into the garage and fire up a joint. I keep the bag out in the garage because I intend on quitting. I would be doing a hit constantly if I kept it inside.

I have plenty of excuses why I shouldn't quit but I won't go into that at this time. It's now 9:15 and I cannot believe how early customers call this office phone. I can't understand why Bill would complain about the sign! I have a special attachment in our contract to install it! He approved the installation and now wants me to fix the holes in place of where he removed it. It probably wasn't that important to him at the time we discussed it and he forgot.

I am sure he will remember once I phone him and remind him of his earlier approval. I put a fence sign on every new fence installation and never had a complaint about it until now.

I need to burn one and get inside and eat my breakfast before I start my day. This is a great start to the day. It calms my nerves and keeps my cool to allow my temper to handle the work complaints. I finished my joint and went inside.

What a great breakfast. The salmon was cooked to perfection and tasted great. I went over to my desk and began to return calls from my messages.

"Bill! This is Shawn. How are you this morning?"

"I see you received my message about the sign."

I have tons of things to do today, Bill. I can't believe you are using my time to complain about a sign you signed for. You approved this with your signature on our contract! I have a hard time believing the sign is so problematic, especially with the location of it! It faces Canal Street. Its location is frequented by about five people daily.

Who will see it anyway?

I can have a crew on the way to your property to replace the two pickets with screw holes in them. However, removing the sign has voided our contract and your warranty. Please put it back and we will forget this conversation ever took place.

I don't agree with you, Shawn, but will review our contract and get back to you. Ok! I know what is in my paperwork and I am sure you overlooked it. Have a great day! Bye!

The next call I made was to Eric, my foreman. I needed to find out what happened down the street with the posts being installed on the neighbor's property. He told me the problem had been solved. He already spoke with Tim and reviewed the survey. The posts were correctly placed on the property and did not need to be moved. Tim made a mistake when reading the survey and had already apologized for being a "crazed" customer. He assured me that the survey was read correctly by my foreman and the work performed was precise and accurate.

I was happy to hear the problem was resolved and it wasn't the fault of my company. If the posts were in the wrong location, I would have been all over Eric. He is instructed by me to thoroughly review the Plat of Survey with every customer prior to installing any posts to avoid mistakes. That's what threw me off because Eric was always within boundaries and made very few mistakes.

I became calmer after my conversation with him. I took a break, and a deep breath. I looked up towards the ceiling and decided to speak with the Lord. I needed to thank him for getting me through these problems.

The best thing I needed to ask him was for his guidance with respect to smoking cannabis. I also mentioned chewing and masturbating when I don't see Cal. I really didn't want to give those up because it feels so fine.

Just thinking about it inspired me to visit my room and do it again. I know it is the high that is making me feel this urge. I couldn't resist it because I was up and ready. My breathing began to deepen as I thought of walking into my room to begin. I tried to come up with an excuse which would excuse me from the office. I looked over to my operations manager and began to think about the first time I met her.

I met this lady named Indigo at a volleyball game I played. I considered her to be a muse. She named herself. It was not her birth name. That day she wrote many pages in my book of life.

After a day or two I began to receive text messages from her. The conversation went as follows.

Indigo- You're hot Shawn!

Response_ thanks! Does that mean you'll camp out with me next week?

Indigo- Of course! Response- just out of curiosity, why did you decide to text me? Why would your first message tell me how hot you think I was?

I received no response for a while and then a message came across the screen that read, "You're also cute to me. I will text you later."

Our relationship was short lived. Indigo liked trying to make me feel bad for having slept with another woman while I was on vacation. I was honest with her with respect to having crossed the line; but it was early in our relationship, and I was quite sure she was not as innocent as her words portrayed.

Our break-up became difficult since she was working with me, but we eventually decided to work together on what was supposed to be a strictly professional level.

I run the business out of my house so to a certain degree "strictly professional" was not as easy as it sounded. I was still attracted to her, we worked well together, and at times like this morning her fragrance is just too much.

I told her I was going to take a private call in my room. I told her I would return shortly.

Within my mind came a vision of the lady at the pub. I started to think of her beauty and long legs. This raised my excitement to another level. As I lay in the bed, I began to pleasure myself slowly. I closed my eyes and dreamed of her touch. It ran across my chest and then lower. The thought was intense. It was getting the best of my feelings. She is the type of person to believe the biggest success stories in history are people who take risks. She encouraged me to take one and I looked her deep into the eyes and said I would. The whole time she was facing me with medium length blonde pigtails, a Green Bay Packer cut-off t-shirt and white cotton "Go Go panties". Within a few moments the dream was over. I was full, like an overflowed river. My bank and hand reunited, and I enjoyed the feeling.

I could not help taking myself to another place. I stood up and sped off to the bathroom to clean up.

I returned to the office. Indigo said, "You're late for an appointment!" It had totally slipped my mind! I picked up the phone and called the gentleman. I explained that I was running behind and I would be leaving the office shortly. The appointment was in Palos Heights. It was a fifteen-minute trip down the road from my office.

I was still a little stoned. I was thankful for the few moments I had to myself. I just walked out of the office and approached the pond outside my door. I stopped for a moment to feed the fish. I thanked God for allowing me the time and thoughts to relax me. In the midst of the moment this riddle came to mind:

MAN'S DISPOSITION

The sighs of my companions are flutes resounding in a choir
As I glide without wings
through rings of many colors The sun's rays polarize my shield.
I am the knight of the sea.
Predominantly gray with white surrounded by sapphire,
My skin glistens in the camouflage of my surroundings.
Listen carefully. . .
you will hear the resonance in my voice
My opponents (fully aware) at the time of the joust.
For stealing man's food, I am often times preyed
Listen carefully . . . I a p p e a r   a s   a L o g o .
Apprehensive in my departure
With the rest of the world.

CHAPTER VI

DELIVER US LORD FROM EVERY EVIL

I sped down Lagrange Road passed a church I used to attend. I began thinking of a short saying the priest used to say after the congregation said The Lord's Prayer. It has the greatest versus, with meaning..."Deliver us Lord from every evil and grant us peace in our day. In your mercy keep us free from sin and protect us from all anxiety as we wait in joyful hope for the coming of our Savior Jesus Christ our Lord. Amen".

I find myself saying the Lord's Prayer followed with this embolism twenty-five to thirty times a day. Sometimes much more and other times much less.

I feel better protected by the Lord and his Angels during and after saying it. It's nice to know I have angels to protect me. The Lord sent them to protect me. They're here. God heard my prayer. I am saved in the Spirit. God is in my heart. His angels accompany me everyday!

I enjoy reciting this everyday. It keeps me better in line and safe from the negative forces.

I found that a bit of prayer or just anything religious used in my day helps me. I try so hard to follow the ways of the Lord. I guess being a sinner is common and I am not alone. This ride down Lagrange Road has its times. There is a crane across the road. It completely blocked all lanes. Not a bit of traffic is getting through. Traffic is slowly creeping around this monster piece of equipment.

The slow traffic gave me time to flirt with some of Orland Park's finest women passing next to me. I smile and give them a wiggle of the shoulder as I listen to some music.

I know besides my handsome smile; my Mustang helps attract some attention. Then again, maybe it is the Eminem music blasting out of the window and the roar of a great engine.

I found myself pulling into a gas station. I decided to get a soft drink, because my lips and mouth are very dry from the weed. I looked into the glass cooler and all I could see was alcohol.

A thought came to my brain about how much alcohol there was for sale in a small gas station.

To my left I spotted water and soft drinks. You would think the display would show soft drinks first versus alcohol. Above the Red Bull is a drink called Sparks. I said to myself that Sparks was an alcoholic beverage. Why is it mixed with the soft drinks? I picked up the can and read the label. It contained 8% alcohol. It looked so good to me that I couldn't resist buying it.

A few moments more of driving placed me at the office of my client. He was a professional man, an attorney. I drove into the parking lot and turned the Mustang engine off. I looked around and saw the entrance; I grabbed my suitcase and a few other papers and exited the car. As I approached the secretary she began to stare. I figured she noticed my shirt. It had the words San Diego printed across it. As I approached the desk, she asked me if I had been there. In the middle of our conversation the attorney appeared from around the corner. Shawn! He said, "Won't you come in?"

I accepted his invitation and followed him into his office. I wasn't there too long. We discussed the terms of his new fence and the addresses he wanted them installed. I thanked him and grabbed my signed paperwork. As I exited the office, I gave the cute secretary a wink and a swift wiggle of my bootie. She kind of smiled and said," See you again, Shawn!"

I decided on the way back to look at some properties. I invest in vacant homes. It boosts my income and during these hard times there are great bargains. I stopped at a few and along the way I visited the properties for the attorneys' fence installs. They didn't seem as large as he described and the work installing the fencing would be quite easy.

I sped home before the rain began to fall. The vigorous taps against the window indicated this to be a bad storm on its way.

I pulled into the drive at home and noticed Indigo's car absent from her spot. I remembered she had to pick up permits in various suburban locations. I exited the car and entered the house. The rain continued to fall, and I decided to cancel the other appointments. It wasn't safe driving in the rain. If I had to survey any property lines, it would be impossible with the rain. I sat at my desk and called them to reschedule. As I was canceling the last appointment, I became aroused again.

I decided to call a sex line. I took out my black book and phoned the best. Every single man has one. I refer to it often but sometimes I am unsuccessful in accomplishing my desires. It is kind of hard to talk, masturbate and concentrate all at the same time. I dialed a particular number and a voice said Lacy here! How may I help you? This was the first time I had heard this voice and it surely sounded fine and sexy. I couldn't help but grab myself as I started the conversation. She was a hot fox and I told her how she excited me and what I was intending on doing. It wasn't anything new to her as she excited me more and more. As she spoke my shank grew harder and thicker. It forced my hand's grip to open as if my fingers were flower petals absorbing the sun's light. My hand grabbed its thickness, and it throbbed in excitement. My heart made a pounding sound as she talked sexy into my ear. Without notice I hung up the phone.

I couldn't do this again. I began thinking of, "Deliver Us Lord From Every Evil." The thought stopped all my actions and I dressed myself. I thought of how hard it was trying to stop this impulsive lust which sets into my brain. However, these calls were more than just that as I knew my phone lines were tapped. Let me just say for now; they were also a bit of a trap. Once again, the prayer and ensuing embolism did the job. I rose from the chair and repeated the verses three or four times until the lust of masturbation left my mind.

I had only one more thing to complete before the end of the day. I had a closing on a property and had to attend. Rain or no rain, I had to be there. It was the only appointment I could not cancel. I didn't want to put that off because I would be walking out with a check and that was important.

The rain stopped as I pulled up in front of my client's house. I knew I was on time. The two elderly folks were out in front of the house. I had all the correct paperwork for their fence order prepared in advance and sitting in the folder on the passenger seat. They greeted me as I walked up to their door. They happened to notice I wasn't driving the

Mustang. One of them asked about it as I approached the walkway. When I stood in front of them, I explained how I would rather drive my Hummer in the rain. It was much safer primarily because of its size. They remarked how they liked the bright color yellow and the writing on the side, representing the business.

This was the second time I had visited their home. It was about fourteen days ago since my last visit. I knew my visit had to be fast and short. Sometimes the more time I spend on other subjects it interferes with the sale itself. I gave my full attention to the contract, getting the measurements correct with respect to their property lines.

I gave each of them a nice handshake and assured them I would start as soon as possible. They were very pleased with my professional way of handling the business intended and I collected the deposit and left.

What nice folks. Two retired senior citizens. The husband was still in great shape even though he had suffered a heart attack not too long ago. I was happy to see him moving around as well as he was. I knew he would be ok, for God healed him. He didn't accept pity from anyone, and he was a strong old man. God bless them was my thought as I left.

While traveling home I made a turn and headed towards an earlier appointment which I had canceled. The rain had now subsided, and I figured the clients might be impressed by my attempt to visit their property. I arrived at their door hoping someone would be home. There wasn't anyone there, so I did some quick measurements, placed the estimate in the mailbox and headed home.

Since I accomplished everything on my schedule, my workday was over. I decided to have another puff of weed. I caught a little buzz. I felt wonderful and very relaxed. The dash lights became dim, and the radio turned off. As I listened to the wind blow my Hummer glided down the road and the lyrics to this entire song came to me:

" THE LIGHT IN YOUR EYES I SEEK "

The only light seen comes from the stars.
You were to me so much more
than I ever thought before.
Now without your touch my hands grow weak.
I haven't felt my own heartbeat!
It's hardly real;
The light in your eyes I seek.
The light in your eyes I seek.

Driving my car down the boulevard.
Dash lights off, no radio;
as I listen to the wind blow.
Ring in my mind till I see our place
where I first felt your embrace.
The curve of your lips, fingertips, to these words I do.
Reminding me of you.

Water caresses the beach where I stand.
The affection you need to feel I truly understand.
The moonlight this night breaking free from the trees;
highlighting the ocean waves
reminding ....me
of the light in your eyes I seek.

My fallen tear is an autumn leaf.
Vision blurred I begin to see...
liquid darkness moving towards me.
I'm on my hands and knees,
 look up at the light and see
your eyes staring at me.
It's the light in your eyes I see.

CHAPTER VII

GOD'S FURRIERY

There was another huge storm front coming my way. I stared at it as I drove towards home. The big black clouds approached. They came closer and were upon me.

I phoned my father and asked him if he had noticed them. I spoke of the huge formations that filled the sky. They appeared as huge chess pieces.

The blackness their shadows created across the evening sky startled me a bit.

The sun became hidden.

The thunder began to roar and caused a tremor. I explained to my father how threatening they appeared and mighty in size.

My father could not see them because all the trees blocked his view. He did mention my mother spoke to him of the extreme darkness outside their home. I explained where I was and with traffic, he anticipated it taking me 20 minutes to arrive at my home in Homer Glen.

God is not messing around this time. I pulled off the side of the road. I took out my cell and captured a still shot. I couldn't stop at just one. I snapped several as the storm passed above me.

The sky was completely blue to the West. I explored the formations and noticed a strange eye in the sky. It was staring directly through me! It had to be an Angel making itself seen! It frightened me slightly. The rain hit the window with intensity. It seemed similar to a shot of whiskey. A total blur of water with each downpour. The wipers sounded as they wiped the windshield. They couldn't keep up with the amount of water falling.

Cling! Cling! The hail Sounded! Singing a horrible song as it hit the vehicle vigorously. They fell angrily on the vehicle leaving indentations on the hood of my driving billboard. The ice balls covered the asphalt, and the pavement became a skating rink before me.

I began speaking to God. Praying like a seven-year-old left alone in a dark room. Please forgive me and save me from my terror. I promised I could and would change!

This storm was sent upon me to frighten me straight! I pleaded with him for forgiveness.

My eyes filled with tears as they glanced across the frightening sky.

The teal green and blackness appeared as a Van Gough painting. The images placed themselves across my windshield.

I heard an Angel voice speak to me. I was told not to worry, for I was safe. The phone began to sound. Ring! Ring! I trembled as I reached to answer it. The voice from above kept talking but I couldn't understand what was being said. The ringing interrupted my attention. It was my father asking if I had made it home safely. He was telling me how furious the storm appeared as the feeling of a hurricane passing.

I answered, "I told you God wasn't fooling around with this one. He really scared the pants off me! I usually don't get scared very easily. I just pulled into the garage, no worries!" I hung up the phone and prepared myself for a bath from heaven. I exited the car and ran for the door. I became wet as the rain consumed me. It fell upon me fast and furiously. I became drenched from head to toe within seconds.

My Diesel racing shoes filled with water as I made my way to the door. The door was locked. I reached for my magnetic key attached to my key ring but I had left them in the ignition as I exited. I remembered the patio door in the back of my house was unlocked so I made my way towards it.

The sky lit up like the fourth of July as the lightning struck the tall pine tree in the back of my property. The force of the blast caused the large tree to slam into the electrical lines prior to crashing to the ground. The electric line severed and was dancing its way towards me like a huge anaconda on steroids.

I closed the sliding door feverishly behind me and entered the pool room. The water from my clothes soaked the floor. The rug became soaked in large puddles around my feet.

I emptied my pockets and began removing my clothing. There I stood in the nude watching the storm continue outside the door. I know Van Gough was hard at work painting this storm with God! I was totally in shock as my body shook.

The electrical line danced with fury prior to the large burst of flames from the transformer.

I decided to call Cali and see if she was ok. I searched for my phone, but it was nowhere to be found. I couldn't understand where I could have put it.

I looked in the pool room, but it wasn't there. I recalled having it in my hand as I pulled up the driveway and into the garage. I figured it had to be in the car and I was mistaken having taken it with me. The smell outside was of burnt plastic as I made my way to the car and searched for my phone.

It wasn't there.

I looked under the seats, on the dashboard and in the rear of the seat. No! Nothing was there.

I went to my office and grabbed the cordless phone. I was surprised to hear a dial tone but dialed my father to ask him which number he had called me on. I couldn't remember which phone I had with me. I have two cell phones which look very similar; one for business and one for personal use. He explained having called my business number.

I went to my desk and grabbed the other phone from the drawer and dialed the number as I walked back into the garage. I did not hear it ringing except from the phone in which I was dialing from.

A few hours had passed and my father phoned again. He was wondering if I had found the phone. I explained how it disappeared. I was puzzled because I had spoken to him just prior to leaving my vehicle. I even checked along the sidewalk. It wasn't in the grass either. I told him I would call him when I found it.

I returned yet again to the garage and took a seat in the Hummer. I found myself thinking about the phone and the day. What have I just experienced? "I asked myself?" I couldn't figure out where the phone had gone. Maybe the angel that appeared before me during the storm claimed it?

There is nothing but silence surrounding me. The only thing I could identify is the dripping water over the gutters surrounding the house. The waterfall in the backyard had quit and was silent. It is the only noise I usually hear when I am in the garage. The circuit breaker must have blown during the storm with the explosion of the transformer.

I was silent with no movement as I sat in the driver's seat of my H2. I began to pray. I brought back my earlier thoughts. "Why is this happening?" I asked God. I went on asking, "What is this all about? What am I to learn from this experience?"

I thanked God for keeping me safe from the storm and taking me home. I didn't know exactly what he expected from me.

On the floor sat a program from a service I had attended last Sunday at church. I leaned over and reached for it. I opened it and began to read the scripture titled, "Confronted By Scripture."

CHAPTER VIII

"CONFRONTED BY SCRIPTURE"

GALATIANS 5:16

So, I say, live by the spirit, and you will not gratify the desires of the sinful nature. For the sinful nature desires what is contrary to the Spirit and the Spirit what is contrary to the sinful nature. They are in conflict with each other, so that you do not do what you want.

But if you are led by the Spirit, you are not under law. The acts of the sinful nature are obvious: sexual immorality, impurity, and debauchery; idolatry and witchcraft; hatred, discord, jealousy, fits of rage, selfish ambition, dissensions, factions, and envy; drunkenness, orgies, and the like.

I warn you, as I did before, that those that live like this will not inherit the Kingdom of God.

But the fruit of the spirit is love, joy, peace, kindness, goodness, faithfulness, gentleness, and self control. Against such things there is no law.

Those that belong to Jesus Christ have crucified the sinful nature with its passions and desires. Since we live by the Spirit, let us keep in step with the Spirit.

My mind is at rest. I gently close my eyes. I felt rested as I took a breath.

I apologized for living in sin. Not being in accordance. For doing things in the natural instead of the Lord's wishes. My body became numb, and I experienced a spiritual orgasm, a sensation from the Lord. I receive Holy intervention and comfort.

My body is no longer mine. My eyes, feelings and my mind are in God's control. I had a strange feeling within me that prompted me to leave Cali. I could no longer see someone who lived in terror and without peace.

She had a lot of baggage; she refused to give it willingly to the Lord. He was strong to protect her and embrace her feelings. She chose to go on in fear and remained with Mr. Mafia. That wasn't for me and my walk of faith. It hurt me to say goodbye. God closed that door, with her company Satan.

A strange force began to pull me from the front seat. It pulled me out the door and to the concrete floor of the garage. I spotted my phone lying beside the weed eater. I laughed at the experience. I knew this was the work of the angels.

I have been directed to live like famous preachers. I like Joel Osteen when he preaches his finest sermon. It's called, "Your Best Life Now!" How inspiring! I love it! It motivated me into this graceful moment. I let my spirit guide me as these words appear:

THE CONTEMPLATION OF BEAUTY

Where lies the beauty ; the shore or the sea

Or does it depend upon where the observer stands

For one lost at sea the intangible is the land

Now does it always depend on where the person be

Is not an ocean more commendable once it is explored

Can the beauty be seen from the outside looking in

If the weather is not clear is not navigation slim

Beauty in water can the sensation truly be endured .

Or in any respect is beauty sincerely appreciated

Does one try to grasp onto what cannot be held

Almost as if a magnetic force is being compelled

Is the history and the present somehow related

Does not her beauty have depth seen through her eyes

Yet the depth in her painting the eyes are not seen

Her like the ocean ; the beauty is everlasting

Trying to hold her as water is probably unwise.

Water flows through the hands is this not the sensation

Can one recognize beauty unless it slips away

To understand entirely this theory . . . if I may "

Is not everything divine sublime to contemplation "

CHAPTER IX

LIFE

OF MIRRORS

Do you believe in a life of mirrors? Life consists of mirrors. You are constantly going back to things you have done before, the same old styles, old friends, old neighborhoods.

These are like mirrors of your life you keep seeing. You sit with backsliding Christians at a neighborhood bar.

The Lord knows you are drinking and sinning. You need to have a good talk to release yourself of this behavior. You don't need people's preaching, or what the hypocrites do. You don't need drinking and running around. You need to get on a solid foundation. Let angels lead you away from the mirrors of life.

Please believe life mirrors create downfalls. They keep you in yesterday. They hold you from finding the treasures God set ahead for you. I can not subject myself to opening up to them. That's why alcohol is called "spirits"; it helps them dig their heels in.

Be skillful, masterful and by doing so you will draw new people into your life. When you've found Christ, you'll learn to say, "I don't feel that way anymore."

Things may look perfect but along the way you find out differently. The ones you love leave you, they begin to lie, and trust is broken. Who do you believe you are? You are a child of Christ, and you behave as such. It is up to you to make that choice and act as his child.

He will watch you grow and never mislead you. We will all be healed but we are at different levels of healing in life.

In the summer of 2008, a friend of mine visited from Wisconsin. I needed his help with some tasks involving the expansion of my business for the spring of 2009.

I hired Indigo full-time as the operations manager and located a second crew.

I just bought a New Holland L-190 skid-steer for the future of the company. I obtained .9 % financing on $42,351.87 with three-year terms.

I purchased a brand-new cedar post turning machine from Dyna Products for $5,500.00 which enables my company the ability to create several unique post tops.

We worked diligently over the course of the winter setting up the newly rented shop and established a line of credit in the amount of $50,000.00.

I signed advertising contracts with Dex One and Yellowbook in the amount of $20,000.00.

We have three shipments of material scheduled to arrive in mid to late March. The first one scheduled to arrive is coming from Cascade Forest Products located in Spokane Washington. In order for me to buy directly from them I had to commit to a full-truckload of material while paying $18,457.13 cash in advance.

The second shipment is scheduled to arrive two days after the first. It is from LR McCoy, a reload facility located in Blue Island, Illinois. This facility is less than an hour from the shop and offers the same quality of material as Cascade Forest Products but they have offered me 45-day terms. So, I committed to a purchase of $12,630.45.

The third shipment is from Kyorichi. This is the first time we have ever ordered a container from China, and we did not know about customs until it was sitting in California racking up dock fees. Indigo worked continuously with customs on this shipment until the container cleared customs and was picked up by a semi-truck driver at the port in Los Angeles. The final bill after bank fees was $17,345.90.

Everything was going according to my plan. My overhead is at its highest and yet I was at my coolest. That is; until the realization sets in. My competitors had plans of their own for my business and it was based upon complete failure.

The 2009 season begins with Eric, my former most trusted foreman, leaving after five years to go with a bigger fence company.

When I learned of this news; I was glad to have hired the second crew. Unfortunately, the second crew also made plans to work for the same fence company as Eric.

I have no crew to install the 25 fences I already had sold and scheduled to install at the beginning of April.

Indigo quit her job to work here with me and my Wisconsin friend has been traveling back and forth each weekend to spend time with his wife and children.

Somehow- I am at peace and trusting God will provide.

The two laborers who have worked with Eric decide not to work for the other fence company. They understand the importance of being the only crew for an expanding company relative to being the 7'th or 8'th crew for a bigger fence company. They are committed to working 70-hour work weeks for Upright Fences and have already made phone calls searching for other people who also want to help this company succeed. These were the plans of the Lord. Good things happen! God Makes a way out of no way!

I obtained a touch of wealth during the 09 season which floored me especially after the way the season started. I am enjoying my new mirrors.

In order for you to understand my new situation I will brief you on positive energy. Don't believe in feeding negative energy. You're wasting time and effort. You'll never accomplish your true heart's desires. Just look to go forward according to plans of life.

You must learn how to pick up on them. God does talk! He is there and you will find him just by listening, praying, and living within the word of the Bible.

You must learn through your heart to give without reason and love without limits. Stretch out and acquire your dreams. They are there and waiting for you in spite of your fears. These are the hallmarks of the divine plan of your life. These are the traits of a superhuman: honor, valor, and courage. If these badges are worn with pride, the unspeakable desires of our heart become reality.

When we open ourselves up in an unconscious state, we become more susceptible to the darkness.

Mostly we will complain and by doing so we will rally the spirits up. Seriously, when we complain or gossip, we rally these spirits up to go out and do something badly or lash out at someone undeserving.

We do it in business, politics and we do it within our own families. We just have not been aware of what we are doing.

The darkened paths will be illuminated with a simple gaze and broken spirits will be healed. Choosing to live by the spirit will not only change your life's destiny but it will encourage others who are in your presence to follow.

This is a time to welcome the greatness of God into your hearts. This is a time for humble prayer.

I developed what I call the PSO mentality in the beginning of the 2009 season. I began to view the world as Predators, Scavengers, and Opportunists.

I could not believe Eric had left my company, especially since I loaned him $10,000.00 as a down-payment on his home so his family could move from Chicago to the suburbs. His children were growing up way too fast in the wrong direction.

I could not believe the owner of the larger fence company deliberately set out to crush my company by taking both of my crews. This owner was considered to be a friend of mine…we used to work-out at the gym together.

I also could not believe how one supplier deliberately attempted to shortchange me. The quality of material from LR McCoy was supposed to have been the same grade of material as Cascade Forest Products. Not only was the material sent to me in poor quality, but they deliberately would turn the 2x4 on the bottom of the skid the long way on 80% of the material ordered from them. They added more money to their top-line by doing this. You see, all of the bundles would appear to be the same height therefore each pallet was billed at 660 pickets per unit. Yet 80% of the skids they sent out had the 2x4 turned long ways on the bottom of the skid and only contained 580 pickets.

I later found out that LR McCoy purchased products from Cascade Forest Products and Cascade Forest Products did not approve of the fashion in which they were conducting business, so they agreed to be a consistent supplier of material for Upright Fences.

For a while I became disheartened. I had a difficult time trusting anybody. I began complaining and gossiping about these occurrences in my life.

Then I realized God had stepped in. He fights the battles for me. No weapon formed against me will prosper. He is my strength.

My brother Tim helped me overcome this PSO mentality I was developing when he shared a story his boss had shared with him.

His boss owned a lumber company in Arizona and at some point in time he discovered a bum living in the lumber yard. The boss began to help the bum and allowed him to sleep inside at night while giving him small projects throughout the day. Slowly but surely more and more lumber began disappearing from the property. The bum had moved on to better things and actually began building modular homes for people with the lumber from the yard.

The owner of the company began assisting the bum with these homes while charging him for the material.

Shortly thereafter, more and more homes were needed to be built but the bum was nowhere to be found.

The owner decided to build the homes himself and to this day is now one of the biggest manufacturers of these homes in the nation. While hearing this short story; I realized not every business owner has this PSO mentality and I was determined to remain a spiritually grounded business owner. Thinking of a couple passages from the bible I found myself in prayer:

Lord, God, Master
I ask for the ability to hear and understand
these parables;
related to my adventures and the way I lived.
The parable of the lamp states that no one lights the lamp
with intentions to conceal the true light it intends to give.
My poetry is my prayer
Everything has become visible with no regrets
and everything hidden; now has become known.
I have felt the vibration of these words,
embraced with a generous and good heart.
My words need to become the root
so others may bear fruit through my own perseverance.
The soil in which we are all placed is rich.
The anxieties, riches, pleasures of life and rues of men;
these are the thorns disabling their perfect adherence.

In a time of trial the sentence of autumn is heard.

The one to whom little is forgiven loves little.

Those that seek to be saved shall be lost.

From the fullness of my heart my mouth speaks

the word which ought to be heard.

Luke 8, 11-17; Luke 9, 24 "No one who lights the lamp conceals it under the bed; rather, he places it on a lamp stand."

Proverbs 10 verse 9 "He who walks uprightly walks securely, but he who takes a crooked way shall be found out and punished."

CHAPTER X

DREAMING WITH AN ANGEL

I woke up early this morning after yesterday's rain. It had tired me. I lay looking towards the ceiling. My mind wondered about the room. I wasn't lonely as much as alone. It is a feeling for all to experience. The quiet in the house surrounds me. The sound of the wind whistles outside through the trees. The more I concentrate on the quiet; the more sound I hear. I lay, listening and concentrating on the peace God developed in my life.

I started thinking about where in life I am. The fabulous places I visited through today. The safety of the Lord took me each step along the way. The journey was great I have to say. I disdainfully know in my heart there is more to come.

I became overtaken with a dream. I had a strange sensation overtake my soul. It took me to another place.

This wasn't any place I could recall at all. I have never visited here within this small space of my mind. There wasn't anything that looked familiar to me.

There were fifteen beautiful women dressed in white dancing. My eyes caught the attention of a few. My eyes encircled just upon one beauty. I began to catch her moods and motions. She danced gracefully across the floor. I lay intensified with her emotions. I lay wondering if she will come to me. I noticed the others lit up a joint. How I wanted to participate. My body began to desire the smoke that exited from the fine rolled paper.

Were they going to notice me? How long could I lay here in silence?

A few moments passed as the light in the dark grew. It flew before me. The fine smoke that each of them exhaled.

A blonde beauty noticed me and lay beside me. She wanted me to place my hand across her breast. I responded as a normal man would. I placed my hand where she had requested.

She looked in my direction. A smile crossed her face. I didn't know her name, but she reminded me of a singer named Britney.

In the distance of my mind, I imagined Britney Spears. She had just laid beside me. She came to me in my dreams. This was the only woman I dreamed of. She was a beautiful woman, as beautiful as the surroundings.

The feeling of her lying next to me sparked a fire through my body. The intense heat of desire and lust ran through me.

I followed the flow of this wonderful river of lust. I looked over to this dream lady and noticed the sparkle of her blue eyes. The highway to her soul showed how pure she was. How delighted was the thought of lying with her.

She began to kiss me as my fingers pressed between the curves of her butt cheeks. She began to gasp for breath and then speak and rise over me. She warned me of my recent stock trade. She said I would lose everything if I did not exit the current trade I was in. I became upset and said "Britney, why would you say such a thing?" Her response was cold as she rolled to the floor saying "this is not Britney! I am just speaking through her."

I was amazed her presence surrounded me here this way. Every situation provides an opportunity. It is up to you to find it.

My eyes closed and the mystery of the happenings overtook me. I felt the warm hand of the angel place the joint into my mouth. I drew on it slowly afraid the intention would be taken away.

As I inhaled; I could feel the high hit my head then rush through my body. I lay relaxed in the beauty of the spirit. My mind created more pictures of pleasure as she began to stroke me. The feeling I was experiencing was intensifying. I felt as if I was in a castle surrounded by beautiful women. I was amazed to be where I was at. It was an unknown place with all the women coming towards me to help her please me. Britney's eyes danced and I felt the urge to pull back. I couldn't let go of the moment.

The spirits increased. They became stricken with my handsome looks. They began to touch me. It was something I never experienced and didn't want to stop. The one called Britney rose and began to dance in front of me. She understood the passion. It was similar to her life and her music, playing in my head. Dancing was her outlet and writing was mine. It was a perfect combination between the two of us.

Still the movements of the others continued. The hands of the angels covered and stroked me. The pleasure became more intense. I decided to just lay there and see how much further this could go. I didn't want to move because I was afraid I would wake up and this dream would be over. I drew on the joint over and over. I enjoyed the beauty that was playing with the sensors of my body.

Through another channel of my mind Cal appeared. Britney was thankful she was in my dreams when it happened. The dancing beauties hid in the closet while Cal and I spoke.

I knew Britney was still here because her slippers were in the doorway. The warmth of her dancing feet filled them.

I jumped out of bed and ran into my office.

Cal looked at me and asked, "whose slippers are those?"

I couldn't answer. Britney wouldn't let the words come out of my mouth. She didn't think it was any of Cal's business.

Suddenly a cab pulled into the driveway and Cal was gone.

Be happy Shawn, she has left your mind. I did that for you. You have many here that desire you without baggage and trouble to await your heart.

Come to us and enjoy our pleasures. I couldn't do it. I stopped like a fast car hitting a wall. I asked her to pray with me.

She knew I needed a break from everything basic. The room became thirty degrees cooler.

There were footprints that appeared strangely across the Pergo floor. The black material on the couch showed the same set of prints. There were three sets of slippers in the doorway. The house began to tremble as I felt uprooted. I found myself in an airplane with Britney. I couldn't imagine where she was taking me.

"Shawn, just stay in the moment with me and enjoy it. We're not in the past or the future," she explained. Look at it as being infostered into a childhood memory if you like!"

While lying on my back I am conscious of the movement of the plane.

"Crash into the wave of the words I say to you nakedly! Nakedly." Shawn says. Although I have not opened my eyes yet; it seems many others are lying on the floor as well. I slightly remember seeing other people fall to the floor after he spoke. The words continue to travel around the inside and outside of the plane ~~~~"No one comes to the Father except through him"~~~~" I am the way and the truth and the light"~~~~

He asks ~~~~"does 'thiz' sound familiar~~~~ his voice sounding more and more like Jesse Jackson or Don King.

I could not help but think of the Hudson River plane. ~~~~"You ask for signs?" ~~~~ His voice becomes more stern with each spoken word.

The s's and z's create this chainsaw-like whip sound and his voice pierces holes through different parts of the plane's compast.

1) "We are all sponge ornaments hanging from a tree. The world is a sponge!"

2) Here you are Mr. Spiritual on one end and Mr. Mafia on the other!

I heard him say these words to me after showing me a quick clip of myself talking to my uncle. In the clip I am all Mr. Machismo. "I wanted to be a made guy!" Yep, I said it.

His voice got loud and excited; it roared fiercer than it had before. I was slightly afraid not to listen to what he was just about to say. I also worried listening may be the death of me. I think I have pushed him as far as I can or could. I think he is pissed.

My hands became numb in an instant and my feet became too hot to stand on. I placed my hands on my feet and began to roll back and forth. Back and forth.

I wasn't breathing. I slightly remember feeling like this two other times in my life. Both times the end result was not good. Not good at all.

I am in a dryer being tossed around at age eleven.

I am in a garbage can about to be rolled down a hill in the wintertime at age thirteen.

Now I am thirty-five. My feet have warmed so much my hands are melting. I am reminded of the wicked witch stewing her boiling pot. I am reminded of the waitress at the Melting Pot in Orlando Florida; she is much better looking than the wicked witch but her hands were still stewing a boiling pot.

Sometimes I have thoughts like this when I am nervous. I think it has only been two or three seconds in which I was talking to myself. Then God spoke to me with clairvoyance.

"Do you remember yelling 'this' to me after your fence crew left you?" God spoke the word 'this' sounding exactly like Cali.

"Thisssssss! I tell ya. This! I tell ya!

Try to do . . . this; while attempting to save the person you love!"

I saw her body all curled up. She is uncomfortable, with heavy expressions weighing on her face. Thissss!!!!! And the s becomes a z and pretty soon the z becomes an s.

"Swishhh!", "Swishhh!", "Swissssh!"

Michael Jordan's hands held down eyes wide open.

All passengers now appear to be seated. Eyes wide open as the holes in the compartment begin to heal themselves right before our eyes.

It seems everybody is afraid to look at me. They probably want to know what I did so badly to have Godzilla come after me. My eyes pierce the entire cabin looking for someway out. Somewhere else I can go. "Like a good neighbor, State Farm isn't there"!

I run to the bathroom and begin to splash water on my face.

"To think for all these years, I wanted to be a made guy. I can understand why God is upset with me. I remember hanging up the phone with my uncle after hearing myself say the words "I wanted to be a made guy!"

I remember telling Cali about the conversation. I remember telling her we are all made guys.

"We are all made guys. Shawn Shawn, I like that!" Cali taps my glass prior to doing the shots. At the time I thought it was a thought I came up with on my own. Now I know differently. Now I know he knows everything about my life.

The splashing of the water does not seem to be helping my temperature at all. My face begins to melt into my hands while I look into the mirror. I try to remember what I yelled at him when my crew left.

~~~~"Do you remember yelling thisssss?"~~~~~ His words categorically searched the events in my mind.

I touched the mirror with my melting hand and my skin became a small image on the mirror. The mirror became a small screen with no sound. The image appearing is the parking lot of my shop.

I am walking from the shop to the southeast corner of the gravel parking lot while staring at the 1957 Yale forklift we had recently pushed just to the edge of the property.

Mr. Photographer. I need a close-up of my words and actions as I fall to my knees.
"WHY HAVE YOU FORSAKEN ME?" rattles the screen until the mirror appears on the wall again.

I realized what he wanted from me and why he persisted I have this dragon-style luck as some have called it. I am surprised that 2011 years have passed and yet I am the one given these thoughts.

The overall consensus has been that Jesus was sent in the form of a human being to die for our sins. He trusted God's voice and was very in tune with living a spiritual life. I believe he spoke his last words for all human beings. I believe Jesus never felt forsaken by God at all. I believe he spoke those words for us.

I picture Jesus hanging on the cross listening to his father's voice waiting to speak.

I picture God instructing Jesus to say those last words.

I picture Jesus knowing how humiliating it may sound coming from his voice.

I see him swallowing his pride once again for us.

"My God, My God, why have you forsaken me?"

I think God sometimes feels forsaken by me.

I think God sometimes feels forsaken by us.

Jesus was here for us. Jesus spoke those words for us. Jesus was instructed to say those words by God. God knew humans would say those words. He knew some of us would even use it as an excuse not to have faith and not to worship.

I believe he no longer wants me to have excuses. I believe he wants no more excuses from any of us.

As I look into the mirror, I hear a song playing through the flight attendants intercom. The last time I heard this song it was right after the storm.

Zissafiss' voice introduces the piece entitled "The Alcohol/Jesus Song "

"I didn't know life without you.

That same life I wanted to forget when I was 22.

I couldn't begin to understand.

We were on the rocks together and you held my hand.

More tightly than any person can.

Much stronger as I became a man.

I couldn't let go no matter how hard I tried.

I saw my reflection as I began to cry;

in the bottom of the glass as I began to ask God- Why?

Then I realized . . .

My life had just begun.

When I saw my reflection. " When I saw my reflection after hearing those words, I decided not to ask God "Why" anymore. Not ever again.

At that moment my reflection became a satellite to our nation. We have been overworked. We have been overstressed. Our personal lives have not reduced the underlying tension which fills most of our houses. Some of our children are dealing with multiple households for parents.

All humans have found some type of glamor associated with being partially right and/or seeing other people finally getting "what is coming to them."

When are we as a people going to admit that we do not know anything at all?

Peace, I say to you! It is this Peace I bring for you!

Things are exactly the way they are supposed to be. They always are!

God's Pace. God'zzz Pace." ~~~~ I could hardly move when the voice stopped. The vibration of the letter s became the letter z.

I walk out of the bathroom and people make eye contact with me. Some smile. Nobody says anything.

There is no indication any of this actually just happened. I want to say something. I want someone to say something.

Not a word is spoken by anyone the remainder of the flight. We took pictures with the cameras of our minds. I see love in the eyes of dolphins. I felt Britney's love and passion for me. I shared the same feelings for her and at this moment I knew Britney was all mine.

We ride the dolphins like companion jet skis. We were inseparable, above and below the water's surface. We had no difficulty breathing on this entire journey.

Two rainbows appeared in front of us and the two dolphins raced each other to the point where the rainbow's colors dispersed in the ocean's body of water. The dolphins race into the bright colors surrounding us. I found myself engulfed within the color of yellow. The stripes of color disappeared into the ocean's horizon.

The two of us blended within the amazing color display which took over the sky. Immediately; I am racing through the brilliancy of the color yellow itself. My body merges and blends with the color. As the dolphin takes a nice deep breath from its blowhole it becomes a whale. Amazingly, the killer whale is actually a big dolphin and has grown tremendously in size relative to me and its skin has become more flexible.

I can no longer see Britney. She had disappeared into the waterline. I tried so hard to find her as I was pulled by a strange force created by the vibrational sounds the color was resonating. It was as if a dribbling basketball was riding the waves of my mind. I found myself dazed and flustered.

I began to think of my life and the situation I am in. I began to thank all the angels for their spiritual guidance but before I could finish a dolphin named Zissafiss came on a commercial. His voice methodically forms a rhythm with the basketball dribbling between his fins.

"You see most of us are just dribbling through our legs in life. Occasionally, we all make a nice cross-over move and actually take a big leap of faith." "Often . . . times though," the ball bouncing back and forth between his fins, "we are just going back and forth. We can have whatever we want so why have you chosen this method of life?"

A television set flashes on and off intermittently until I see myself on the 42" plasma. Everything I see myself doing is up-side down. Literally, my feet are at the top of the screen and my head at the bottom.

Zissafiss continues . . . "water is amazing; it has the ability to take any shape or carve any shape through mountains. It also has the ability to read and understand.

For years people have believed the brain is responsible for methodical thinking and creativeness. For years our beliefs have been misguided. The brain is simply an obstruction between God and yourself. Wear a baseball cap and the obstruction gets worse. Turn it sideways and bounce it back where it came from. Our hearts are connected to God. We are sponges. Many experienced the capabilities of a human being whose heart was fully connected with God 2011 years ago.

Zissafiss is dribbling the ball faster and faster between his fins and the images get bigger and brighter on the screen.

Creating a wave of newer images popping up. I was stuck between the colors of the rainbow and the surface of the ocean itself. The sound of the dribbling basketball orchestrates simultaneously with me as I begin to travel with explosive force riding forward and backward over the entire rainbow.

It happens so quickly there is not enough time to get scared especially since the pauses between rapid movements occur just long enough for me to catch my breath. I am quite dizzy yet trying to get my bearings about myself.

The sound of the dribbling basketball has almost disappeared and is easily replaced with a very direct speaking voice: "There are many dolphins with riders, but great distances separate them from one another… I am the 'Shoemaker' of the dolphins."

I am now in between the surface layers of the ocean and the bands of the rainbow. I am circling around on a magic carpet of water in between those vibrational frequencies. I realize the ground and the water still have root of me based upon the series of water sprites having formed the magic carpets…one of which I am on. I wonder if Britney was experiencing the same sensations. I wonder if she is in a different color experiencing something entirely different than me.

A crystallized BraveHeart voice captures my spirit while hearing the words "We are all just up here doing circles!"

~~~~"Nothing about this life is typical. Nothing at all is predictable. I can't take it anymore. We are all wearing lace and leather or something in between. We are confused as a society. We have not until recently been as open and as vulnerable either.

Thankfully, somehow at our weakest; we are our strongest! There are no rational explanations for this type of confidence. Those with faith understand entirely. Hopefully you let go a long time ago and now fly with the angels instead.

The magic color of the rainbow overtook the blue of the ocean. There were carpets of color spread over the waves. They tripled in size with the explosion of color. A number of dolphins are circling in the air within the rainbow's atmosphere now.

My circular direction stops.

Tankashor.

Out in the distance I spot Britney flowing over the rainbow. She was taken out of my dreams and into the heavens. She was never to be seen in the dream again.

The sadness of it all overtook me and I wanted to wake up but couldn't. I feel the band of light refracting from the rainbow and into my belly button. I feel as if I am an object being placed into the back of a flexible slingshot. This band of light mirrors the rainbow and soon I find myself completely under water. I went deeper and deeper into the water line in front of me.

A sign saying "Start Again" is chiseled into the side of an abandoned ship. The ship is upside down and I am trying to read its name, but I am accelerating to a tremendous speed within seconds. A speed I am sure I have not experienced before.

Nascar hasn't even experienced speeds like this before. Nasa hasn't either.

Zissafiss had swum directly under me and lifted me onto him. He gained speed as we flew over the water tips of color. The fish below appeared in different colors as we rode over them.

I exit the water just long enough to take a deep breath prior to hitting the water again with explosive force.

I have just completed one big circle and the "Start Again" sign appears again in front of me. I feel as if I am traveling in the color yellow band; first in a circular direction. Then back and forth like being pulled in two directions of a slingshot.

I am stretched within the band to a point near the "Start Again" sign. I am completely submerged underwater and for the first time I am having difficulty breathing. My ears begin ringing with tremendous force. I am launched in a forward direction and my stomach cannot do anything except upheave the last two days of fruits and vegetables.

The separation of the water continues in front of me. It reminds me of the Bible when Jesus allowed the opening of the Red Sea as Moses and others crossed. The same thing was happening here as my body tossed from side to side with more force than any wooden roller coaster has ever tossed me around.

I could see the floor of the ocean and everything else disappeared. There was no vegetation. Not even a dead fish appeared alone. Where was I in this dream? Where is this secluded location? I began to feel the sand of the ocean floor beneath my feet. There are drops of Jupiter everywhere and landing in different places surrounding me.

Little by little objects begin to emerge from the layers of sand which include: Chariot boxes, four, six, and eight spoke chariot wheels, horse and human skeletal remains all silently appear as a testimony to the Miracle of the parting of The Red Sea. Each individual drop embraces the next and water rings begin to form. The dolphin has disappeared.

I find myself standing in a waterfall. I am looking up towards the light. I can hardly think as the water continues to fall around me without touching my body at all. The water is mixing with the colors of light.

"Turn your life around Son!" The voice of God is more deliberate than ever. All movement seems to stop except for the magic carpet of water flowing beneath me. The yellowish and silver strands of water run quickly beneath me and further extend in multiple directions all around me. I feel like an octopus.

I saw silver streams of light surrounding my cat and soon the laptop and calico cat merged together as one. I saw a peace sign being written in the sky by an airplane. I soon saw the words "Jesus loves you" to follow.

One by one, stone tablets form in front of me. They are massive and beautiful. The tablets read:

Take a leap into faith Shawn!

Start Again

Change Yourself

So Many of Us Never Do

The tablets and the written words begin circling my body creating a feeling of dizziness. I try to stand up too quickly and my head becomes lit with light. My eyes open.

Britney is playing in the background and the people in the tavern have all gathered around me. I notice four plaques on the wall, but my eyes are fixated on the one that reads "Start Again". At the same time the woman holding me is asking me to start my story again. I begin to tell everyone about being stranded on the highway.

I begin to tell them about the car at the bottom of the hill. "There was no driver when I got in the backseat!" I picture the arm grabbing the steering wheel just before the curve.

It's the last thing I see. The face of Britney appeared; she reached for my hand and returned me back to my room.

She asked me if I had seen the sign on the ship which read "Start Again!"

CHAPTER XI

BELIEVING

IS SEEING

I decided to take the entire day off. I wasn't doing anything in the office. The past days were exhausting and I felt drained. I had no enthusiasm to do anything. The only thoughts that crossed my mind were those of the dream. It was so unusual and scary to me. It was a reality check that set me into a new motion.

My family and friends have been saying I am under too much stress and thought the dream was my mind's way of telling me to start fresh. I am, however, confident enough to know that I am not hallucinating. These conversations with God and Britney are real.

I do not think anyone truly believes these experiences are happening in my life to the detail I am describing but I understand how difficult it must be for them.

The easiest way the angel explained it to me was like this:

"Do you know how you sometimes hang out with somebody and after being with them your energy levels are drained? They are what we angels sometimes refer to as a 'downer'. Well, those types of people are probably not daily associates with let's say a spiritual guru. However, if the 'downer' decides to call the spiritual guru; the spiritual guru will most certainly set aside some time to try and visit with and tend to their needs."

"Are you following me so far?" the angel asks.

"Yes, I am. I think you are basically saying there are people who do not like to socialize with other people but if the other people call them- they will indeed help them out in some way. (At least by having a conversation with them)" Shawn says. "

You are correct so far." The angel flaps and adjusts her left wing as she continues "they are not any different than you and me!"

Shawn interrupts. "No, they are much different than you and me! We talk all the time. We are friends. I am offended that you would say those words to me!" Shawn's voice sounds more than frustrated. "You are just like everyone else, and you take our friendship for granted!"

The angel takes a couple of steps backwards and runs forward kicking me in the balls.

A loud groan roars from my lips "Why" Why did you just do that?"

"Because you are a dumbfuck! You mind as well name a chapter in your book just that; Dumbfuck!" the angel yells out.

I recall being scared when this was happening.

"Don't do that again!" Shawn yells.

The angel takes a step back and delivers another kick. This time I turn to the side and allow the kick to catch my upper leg. The angel's foot connects directly with the sciatic nerve.

I catch the angel's leg with my left hand, and I look into her eyes and ask, "Now what?"

The angel standing on one foot decides to blast me directly in my lower lip and chin with her fist.

I sweep the angel's one leg out from underneath her and the two of us fall to the floor. I begin choking the angel and yelling "Is 'this' what you want from me, is 'this' what you want?"

The angel gasps for breath and begins crying.

"I told you they are no different from us!"

I begin to release the grasp of my hand from her neck. I hear my words echoing within the closet... "Is 'this' what you want from me? Is 'this' what you want?'

I am told "I sounded like a nigger saying it."

I see the slippers in the doorway.

I picture Cali struggling to hold the weight of her cousins' weight from the hanging rope.

There were hours of screaming afterwards. The word "dumbfuck" was used at least thirty times. I could not argue back. I was patient. I was calm.

The taxi cab driver was told he was not needed anymore.

The angel came back into the bedroom and began laughing while saying "I can't believe I have to kick you in the balls to make this statement but you deserve it!"

I did not know where she was going with this conversation and honestly, I am hesitant to stand directly in front of her.

I found myself turning slightly acute to protect my "manhood".

The angel says "Shawn Shawn, how easily you provoke. I was happy to see you calm down and not freak out any further towards me but let this be a lesson learned by you."

"A lesson? I do not know who you are right now and honestly, I am a little scared!" Shawn replies.

"Do you remember me saying they are no different than me and you?" The angel asks.

"Yes, I do. You said there are people who are 'downers' and other people do not like to be around them. You compared me and you with them!" Shawn replies.

"Okay and what I was trying to say is pretty simple. Angels view most humans as 'downers' and occasionally these 'downers' will call upon us and we will respond to help their needs."

The angel continues "Shawn, you however seem to call upon me a lot, so I am here a lot! Therefore, our relationship is quite different from the average human/angel relationship. I love you, Shawn. Your belief is powerful. You're still human though and you're too easily provoked.

'Every situation provides an opportunity- you just have to find it'."

"Now I can't go around and call everyone "dumbfucks" and I can not explain to them why an angel would do such a thing like kicking me in the balls. It is a blessing though. It's a situation that provides an excellent opportunity for growth for all humans.

Angels and God are not on our frequency. We are "downers" to them. We have disappointed them. We have failed to see their intrinsic value their presence will have on our lives if we follow it.

We do not call upon them enough.

We are humans for a reason; different than most may believe and think.

Sometimes we have to get kicked in the balls hard enough just to listen to their points they are making in our lives. Sometimes the kick in the balls is the point. We need to be humbled sometimes to have great faith.

I picture the wings of the angel folded-up underneath her back while my hand grasps her throat. The un-hung mirrored painting lay broken on the closet floor. Her skin sliced three times just above her left wrist. The wounds heal quickly while she pulls the broken pieces of mirror from her flesh.

She begins yelling and screaming at me. She is trying to provoke me more. When she swears, I feel a shield forming around me. The shield deflects her spoken words back in her direction.

"Dumbfuck! Dumbfuck! Dumbfuck!" The shield becomes my badge of honor. I do not argue back. I do not scream. Her own words shake her soul.

"Congratulations Shawn. Wear your shield with pride" the angel speaks her last word to me.

I often think about that experience. I can't believe Britney listened from the closet in the other room while it happened.

The slippers are no longer anywhere in my house.

"I remember when I lost my mind. There was something special about that day." Realizing I was not in control humbled me enough to call upon the angels on a regular basis.

They became my armor. They surround me because I ask them to. They protect me because that is what angels do. Angels are at a higher frequency than us humans because we are "downers" to them. I call upon them more and more.

The more and more I ask; the more and more I learn.

The angels in my mind explained this to me just right. They stated the correct words for the situation. They corrected my ways and the people I associated with. I was to choose my company carefully from here on in. It was the sign of the times. I couldn't go on with Satan and his followers. I made up my mind; it was the Lord's way or nothing.

I stood in shock as the angels floated away and left me in pain. I guess I understand how God is left like I. The kick in the balls is similar to the same pain God experiences when I sin. It doesn't feel good and hurts a lot.

Dreamality is not much different than "The Secret" because we all have the gift of creating our surroundings. "The Power of Now" is amazing if we remain focused in it.

Dreamality forms little by little as we call upon the angels. "The Secret" is not unfolded until and unless God is at the forefront.

It is the angels and it is our focus on God which allows the doors to open in our lives.

The patio door opens. My mom asks "Shawn, are we still going?" "Sorry mom, I lost track of time. Give me a minute to freshen up a bit."

Tonight, is the night of the healing which happens to fall on my grandmother's birthday. I remember reading the email from my mom. I remember seeing the words"

"The main reason why I know you have to go to this healing is the spiritual message I received. Today is your uncle John's birthday and as you know he was my mom's second son, and you are my second son." 22

The negative forces have been trying to deter me from going tonight. I do not hear the phone ringing because my mind is preoccupied with the events of the last few days for me. My mom has been calling to make sure I am ready. I am running late already. The church is not where we thought it was. The coffee spills on my brand-new jacket.

We find the church and although we arrive late the service has not yet started. The priest is running late himself. {God's Pace}

The ceiling is at least fifty-five feet tall and from the center hangs a beautiful cross.

The cross is massive and the impact it has on me while viewing it is amazing.

I stare at the body of Jesus.

The music starts. There is a half hour of prayer and meditation prior to being asked to gather around the altar. We are asked to picture Jesus administering the healing since it is the spirit of Jesus working through the priest.

I stand in front of the altar and the spirit of Jesus approaches me.

He speaks five words and I immediately feel his presence fill every cell in my body. I fall directly backwards and lay on my back in a deep trancious state:

I am encouraged by the spirit to take a break from smoking weed and chewing tobacco.

I feel peace for the first time in a while.

The sounds of the waterfall echo off the walls of the church.

His hands are outstretched. His shoulder muscles are grimacing.

I see Cali struggling to hold the weight of her cousins' body.

I see the gripping rope. I see the only two things helping support Jesus' body from falling.

They are his two feet nailed to the cross. I see his two hands.

I still lay on my back as Jesus talks to me. He speaks of the great flood as images race in my mind. I see the "Start Again" sign. I see the capsized boat. I see his two hands and two feet. I see two of every creature walk unto the ark. (Deuce's Wild)

I see the rainbow, the dolphin, and the magic carpet of water. I see the plasma globe spinning slower and slower until it becomes the earth.

I see the book floating in the bathtub after my seizure.

I see Jesus smiling and walking on water towards me.

CHAPTER XII

THE

SLOW ECONOMY

I walk back into the office overwhelmed by the blank jobless board. I am overwhelmed by the petty circumstances which allocate mine and Indigo's time. I seem to have more tedious things which need tending too but the job board remains empty. Mostly I have become more physically exhausted and more spiritually shoved along.

The glimmers of hope and rays of light have penetrated my body. I wait for the outcome.

I wait for the bank's decision. The Harris representative begins to speak "The business model looks good, the credit is just as strong, but at this time the $200,000 in assets along with a lien on your property is sufficient for us to loan you $80,000.00. Plus, we are going to eliminate this $50,00.00 line of credit you have secured with just your signature.

The loan had entered into its final stages three days ago. At that time, the Harris representative was sure it would be approved without my house needing to be included in any fashion.

Things have changed once again.

I have at least $40,000.00 in equity in my home at a low evaluation. My assets are worth more than the remaining $40,000.00 to me.

The loan is for expansion. It is meant to keep people employed here. I am not sure if these people are worth risking my home for.

I see my funds dwindling to pay their salaries. I see the banks refusing to loan me any further funds next year. I find myself giving it one more month. My personal finances have been paying for Indigo's salary for months now.

I did not expect this decision from the bank.

He says, "I am the way, the truth, and the life. No one comes to the father except through me. My father judges no one, but has committed all judgment to me. All should honor me just as they would honor the father. He who does not honor me does not honor the father who sent me."

The swish sound permeates the room. Tears fill my eyes as I walk in the direction of the pew where my mom is seated. Prior to getting there; a lady offers me a bottle of water. I drink the entire bottle of water and my body is shaking terribly.

"Are you okay Shawn?" My mom asks.

"Are you okay Shawn?"

I have difficulty responding but shake my head as if to say I am okay. My legs shake uncontrollably back and forth for at least five minutes.

I can not believe how powerful this healing is. I wonder if my legs are shaking this much because my sciatic nerve is healing.

I do not know what to think.

Three days have passed since the healing experience and I have been praying often.

I have difficulty sleeping tonight and have not heard a response from my angelic friends.

I beckon for them to return and I collect my thoughts.

Shortly thereafter I hear a beckoning howl from outside my house. It is at least 3:00 A.M.

I open the back door and hear an animal yelping. I throw on my winter gear as fast as I can and run into the silence of the cold night. My breath is apparent in front of me. As I look around, I notice two wolves circling a Siberian husky.

I am standing on a hill highlighted by the moon. I yell with aggression not saying any words "kikikikyigh". The sound distracts the wolves just enough as the husky runs between them both in a southward direction. The wolves head east; they are racing towards me.

I run as fast as I can without looking back and slide the patio door open and close it as quickly as possible. I do not recall the last time I ran as fast as I just did.

Fingertip size bruises have formed on my quadriceps.

The healing begins.

Two days before Halloween and two days after the spiritual guide attempted to contact me.

The spiritual guide I have named Darth has now taken a seat at the podium. Her voice begins to resonate, and she asks; "is there anyone out there connected to Al Capone?"

My great grandfather used to run with Al Capone.

Of course, I should raise my hand.

My spirit comes out and warns me "No! You should not, keep those hands down. There are still a couple of spirits I am uneasy with here in the room!"

I listen to my spirit and do not raise my hand.

She has called for an assistant to join her on stage now since nobody else in the room seemed to connect with the Al Capone entity. Her voice becomes distracted. She is fumbling her words. She looks at me and realizes I am reading her mind too.

I know why I elect not to raises my hand when the spiritual guide asks, "Is there anyone in the room who can associate themselves with the word Amber?" My spirit is not 100% comfortable as she continues to speak until the vision of Amber's eyes engulf my soul. Flashback reels of our past Frisbee games and walks enter my mind.

I also know there are 137 people who have gathered in the small church and not one of them raises their hand in association to the word Amber either.

I am not sure why the spiritual guide elects to say "Amber Alert Halloween Night" but she has. I am not naïve enough to believe these experiences as random sets of events.

They are signs and believing is seeing them.

The signs become more apparent. The signs I see while driving towards my house begin to flash and buzz my brain.

I am hungry, a little on edge, and constantly seeing images overlapping the cars while I drive home. I see a white van parked between three pine trees. Running away from the pine trees are at least 50 stuffed animals.

I feel like I am hallucinating. The stop signs are deflecting forward and backward. I gauge my stopping point to be from the one in the middle.

My equilibrium is way off while existing my car and making my way around the back of my house. I scurry to the computer and see an email from my mom. I understand now why I felt so inclined to check my emails. My mom must have really been sending out a vibe to me.

Sagittarius (Nov.22-Dec. 22) Don't get frustrated by the feeling that nothing is going on around you. Something is most certainly brewing, but like a train that rumbles on the outskirts of town, you have to stay still and keep your ears trained for the vibrations. Subtlety is key.

While looking at the 17" monitor I see two numbers repeating themselves after Nov. and Dec. I real (eyes) for the first time in at least 20 years of reading horoscopes those numbers are 22 and 22.

Sagittarius (Nov.22-Dec. 22)

Goosebumps have covered my body entirely. I can not focus at all. Something is happening and when it happens- I have learned to just relax and enjoy. I am not sure how long this spiritual orgasm lasted. I am not sure if it was three minutes or thirty.

The goose bumps deflate with the email box as I close it. My head seems clearer. The next email I see is from Indigo. The subject of the email is named "FOCUS" and I recall her having sent this in response to my email after she and I broke-up.

…"You also get these interesting ideas during meditation and your brain keeps going and going…but from one day to the next it changes so much you sometimes don't go through with a thought or idea. FOCUS on you and getting to know you and doing what you want for your future. FOCUS on your thoughts and make sure that your actions are on track with them. FOCUS on following your dreams. I think you are right and we can still work well together. Thanks for sharing your thoughts with me. In time, when I have time- I will discuss this further with you."

As my mind begins to FOCUS on the screen in front of me, I can not help but fall into a deep meditational state. I am asking God the purpose and meaning of the spiritual guides message the other night.

I know Cali and I had problems with Mr. Mafia, her ex-boyfriend. However, I do not know our lives will be in jeopardy in a few days.

The small hill in my backyard where Amber is buried has gone unfinished now for two years. When I buried her there, I promised to complete that area of my yard prior to finish anything else on the property.

I have been working very hard. When I am not working, I just do not feel like working on anything else but my book.

Nothing; and I mean absolutely nothing has been done on my property in two years either.

The stickers still remain on the skylights. There are fragments of blue tape left on the ceiling. I remember the paint peeling as I pull the 3m tape down.

The Bosch "point of use" water heater has very little "point of use" since the hot water becomes cold while showering. I figure it to be an attempt on my sanity, so I do not allow it to frustrate me. I bought it to conserve energy, but little did I know it was going to attempt to steal mine in order to do so.

The drainage tile the Will County inspectors told me "in no way can it be septic… it is running way too close to your well". You guessed it; it is septic. Since I connected my downspouts to the drainage tile; the stench in my backyard is sometimes awful. The connection happens to be located beneath 600 Sq. feet of stamped concrete and is impossible to repair without great expense.

I am being sued by the Health Department even though I received their approval for the location of the addition, passed every inspection, and called them out to my house to file a complaint. The inspectors gave me the approval to connect my downspouts to the drain tile.

The laws and loopholes of our society.

A judgment was found against me in the amount of $63,000.00. I guess that's why you only see lines at courthouses in a "Slow Economy".

The multi-connected smoke detectors still have the pink plastic bags over them. I decided to use the pink plastic bags because I was afraid to use the 3M tape anywhere else after it had peeled the paint in every area it was used.

The small hill in my backyard sits adjacent to a three-year-old mulberry tree. Amber is buried in the uppermost portion of the hill.

I think Amber got sick of waiting for me to finish the landscaping around her. Hundreds of pink flowers have formed surrounding her grave. Directly above her grave; a rainbow wreath has formed. I am sure I have not seen something as amazing as this before.

The vine appears in a rainbow shape and both ends fasten tightly to the dirt below. I remember holding Amber tightly in the pool; my eyes staring deeply into hers. My love was so deep for her; I consider holder her under the water to prevent her from seizing any further.

The rainbow wreath dances with the song entitled Storm by "Lifehouse" and Amber begins to speak with me. I grab my video camera for proof of what I am experiencing.

"I know you didn't bring me out here to drown.

So why am I ten feet under and upside down?

Barely surviving has become my purpose.

Cause I'm so used to living underneath the surface.

If I could see you; everything would be alright.

If I'd see you… this darkness would turn to light.

To the average person just seeing the video, I am sure the angel dust flying in the air is superfluous. I am certain the guy crying and singing is certain to be having a nervous breakdown. Thankfully the wind chime calms my nerves.

I am also certain Jesus was speaking to me through Amber and these lyrics. I have not been the same ever since hearing him singing these words:

"Barely surviving has become my purpose.

Cause I'm so used to living underneath the surface.

If I could see you, everything would be alright.

If I'd see you… this darkness would turn to light.

And I will walk on water.

And you will catch me if I fall.

I know everything will be alright.

I know everything is alright!"

The forefathers of our country had no problem associating this land with God. So why does this land have a hard time associating with him?

God is barely surviving in our country. His name even appeared on the edge of the coin for a year or so. Some students in Vermont should not be forced to say or hear the words "One Nation under God" but those that want to say it can go to the second-floor gymnasium.

Let's go to the second-floor gymnasium for a minute.

God is speaking there.

1) "If you are not in control, it doesn't mean you're out of control. Control is within your hands and your mind.

2) Your intellect is first within your heart. Then second within the mind. Do not allow it to interfere with your heart's desires. What you have to do is say, Yes! There is no need to worry about how. Or even when! How is up to you or better worded, Me!

3) I believe deeply, within your heart all things are possible.

4) They are plans for your life. These plans are in detail, and you should know. In other words, I am . . .I am the way, the truth, and the life. No one comes to the Father except through Me.

If I'd see you; this darkness would turn to light. And I will walk on water…I did it before!"

As the song finishes the wreath dances in harmony with the wind chime. The song repeats and tears create pathways along my face. The spiritual orgasm has ended. The bruises on my leg are warm to the touch.

The giant carpet of wave beneath my boots reminds me of "The Big Wave" in Mission Beach California. "The Big Wave" is a bar which has this ride I believe it to be called 'Flow Rider'. My vacation seems like it has been months ago. I was more scared then than I am now. Plus, I am not losing my balance every third second and crashing to the water's surface.

Although water has just mysteriously formed underneath me; I feel guided.

I am led to the music. I am led to the words: "Live like you were dying! Like tomorrow was a gift, and you got eternity to think about what you'd do with it. An' what did you do with it? An' what can I do with it? An' what would I do with it?"

The words continued to echo throughout Messenger Woods. The message was clear for me today. The messages have been clear for years.

The business is draining me of my sanity.

My sanity steps in.

I begin to realize how spiritually gifted I am. These experiences have been pulling vital energy from my being and my being is no longer going to accept it. The spiritual guides stepped in.

The angels depict a frightening scene. Deep underground water streams have violently merged together in the sky.

The deer aggressively attack the hunters, and the coyotes join in.

More underground streams rocket through earth and aggressively shatter six-foot diameter tree trunks.

The earth becomes a big aquarium. The sharks are hunting business men.

I also did not expect to be seeing it as a blessing. Believing it is happening for a reason is difficult at this time.

My faith remains strong. I trust in the Lord's plan for myself. I am giving it a month.

In the meantime, I am asking his direction. The angels have guided me here and are surrounded by Sister Dorothy- my pre-school teacher, my grandmother-"Pineapple", and Amber, my pit-bull lab.

Immediately, I feel the urge to get out of the house.

I am walking in Messenger Woods. Cali used to love walking here with me. Her presence and the presence of the other angels continue to surround me.

I am approaching a fork in the path accented by roses. I remember the spiritual reading where Cali was told her grandmother was guiding her. She had two choices and one was good and the other was bad.

She chose Mr. Mafia.

I choose to go right along the path and immediately feel the presence of my grandmother walking with me.

In the distance I hear a song playing. The music and voice is silenced in the leaves of the trees before they reach me. Somehow, they still do.

I know I am meant to hear the words playing and before I can run; my body is being pushed. My feet skid out from underneath me, and a giant wave pool of water rattles the boots I am wearing.

My grandmother had purchased these boots for me right around the same time she purchased the Chinese star. Both have lasted for years.

The levels of the words become deeper and deeper.

The capsized ship looks like the remnant of Noah's Arc.

The signs are everywhere-

"Start Again!"

Chinese templates appear describing a catastrophic flood which covered the whole earth.

The open book, by Huai Nan Zi in 200 BC, floats across the water, "legend states that in ancient times, the poles (North, South, East, and West) that supported the roof of the world were broken."

The heavens broke and a continental shift has occurred. The nine states of China split.

In the midst of the global calamity, a hero by the name of Nuwa appeared and sealed the flood holes with colorful stones.

He approaches me with eight members of his family. The ship comes to rest at the base of the mountain. Pairs of every kind of bird, animal and creature slowly appear.

He shows me symbol after symbol and direct correlation after direct correlation. The ancient Chinese characters reveal a similar story as Noah's Arc. I see a symbol for the world and everything in it. It is in the middle of a crossroad. The symbol stops moving. I see our world stop moving in less than three years.

I see the open book, by Huai Nan Zi in 200 BC, floating towards me across the water.

It comes to rest at the base of my foot.

I bend down to pick it up. The book is completely soaked, and the images soon begin to run off the pages.

Literally! The words formed little legs and arms and ran off the page. Each page turned did the same thing. Some of the pages I saw where like little Halloween and Santa villages.

The words run off every page.

I close the book and stare at the front cover while it transcends into a mosaic type painting.

Immediately I have a flashback of my seizure in the bathtub. The book now rides a wave in the tub like a professional surfer on Hana, Hawaii.

The book: I was holding at the beginning of this episode is soaked. I am sure it has some further meaning then I am prepared or willing to decipher at this time. I have made my way in front of the fireplace still in the bathroom. My naked body rests on the heated tile floor.

I am awake and am surprised to see Nuwa in the bathroom of my house.

I finally understand what all these spiritual messages have been about. The haze begins to fill the room again.

This is only the second time the bathroom has ever steamed up this much, the ceilings are too big and open into the next rooms. I should know; I designed the place.

Nuwa walks towards me and divides himself in half while taking military style steps towards me. The steps are slow and deliberate. 1/1, 2/2, 3/3, and 4/4.

The Japanese and American voices…they were Chinese!

There are now two of them standing in my bathroom.

Nuwa and Noah. Deuce's Wild. The raven and dove return.

CHAPTER XIII

RAVEN

It felt like 150 days while the two of them stood there and conversed with me the importance of who we are as a people. One American and one Chinese man both sharing a similar story about a catastrophic flood for both races.

The flood was not really a flood at all, it was a series of frozen or busted water mains. Not the ones humans create either. They describe the earthy water main breaks as "downright horrific as the water burst upward out from the earth."

God commanded the earth to absorb the water and the portions slow in obeying became salt water in punishment and so became dry and arid. The water which was not absorbed formed the seas thus the flood still exists.

Two rainbows have formed within the walls of my lofted bedroom and Noah and Nuwa are at each end. Each of them holding something in their hands as the two voices speak in Chinese and American to me: "Many people are like this raven! Many are like this dove! All will see the beauty while they are away."

The birds are released and fly into the open air as the vaulted ceilings disappear.

The extent of the rainbow widens, and God's voice shatters the atmosphere. "I was grieved once before by humankind's actions and my heart felt much pain. Humankind still has not realized one important thing" his voice begins to settle a bit . . . "human beings are like these birds- and all of you will eventually return."

The rainbow ascends higher in the sky. Nuwa and Noah stand directly under the ends of the rainbow and a tunnel of light appears connecting the earth and the rainbow itself. Nuwa and Noah are immersed in the light and suddenly the earth floor shifts, and water burst through the earth at each of the rainbow's ends.

Nuwa and Noah stand directly within the flow of this water stream and their bodies are untouched as the racing water and combined colors of light become the "Jewel of the Serengeti".

The lilac breasted roller displays an almost unbelievable palette of colors. Flying straight up for thirty feet, then turning and diving sharply down again, leveling off its flight and 'rolling' its body to the right and left. This display is repeated as many as six times in a matter of seconds.

I stare at the photograph. It is hung on my wall. Nuwa and Noah have disappeared. Although we discussed much, I fail to ask them how exactly the two of them were possible.

I am still not sure today if this means there was more than one flood or if these different stories both came from one offshoot.

I do know there were two of them standing in my bathroom. The steam remains well after they have left.

I try to recall most of what is discussed with Nuwa and Noah and I immediately start taking notes and drawing images for further use when trying to write the book. The chapter names are given to me on tablets I read after seeing the sign "Start Again".

I see the twelve disciples: Judas-his most trusted friend, holding the money bag and resting his elbow on the last supper table. I see Jesus being betrayed by him with a kiss. I see Madonna kissing Britney. I see the Sicarii mob. I see the sword piercing the side of Jesus.

By far one of the coolest things, I remember seeing is Jesus' response to Thomas when he asked for further evidence of the Ark's existence: Jesus responded by temporarily resurrecting Noah's son Ham from the dead. Noah made a pair of hogs appear from under the elephant's tail (they were used for excessive dung removal).

Noah made a pair of cats appear from the lion's nose to deal with the stowaway rat.

According to Ham, Satan got on the Ark last disguised as a donkey.

As the steam escapes the room I am drawing the final image I can remember. It became the image on the front cover of this book.

Noah and Nuwa appear as sponges. Almost like little "SpongeBobs" just before disappearing into the rainbow itself.

My body will not move. The refractions of light seem to be hitting thousands of crystals along the path my feet are frozen in.

The back of my knees are shattered with the force of a baseball bat and I fall directly to my knees.

I have never seen this man before, but he appears to be outraged.

I know I have just shit in my pants somewhere between the fifth or sixth inning as the bat continues to swing.

My body seems to be absorbing the blows pretty well actually. I make the sounds as if I am being hurt by what is happening, but I am amazed this shield has formed around me again like this.

It is a similar shield as the night the angel called me a "dumbfuck" after having kicked me in the balls. I remember those words refracting directly back at her. She was impressed I was capable of doing it so well.

She trained me for this "Southside ass whopping" and the shield was unbelievable.

I am surprised the gentleman stopped when he did but the pool of blood, I am laying in must seem pretty sufficient. With one last kick to the head, he shouted "Cali was an alcoholic anyway; hope she was worth it!"

He left me for dead. Zissafiss appears to me and says "God's Pace for your life is entirely up to you. You may come with me now or you can live with me in eternity forever after you have lived this life to the fullest. Read what you have written, experience life like no other but always know the raven eventually returns."

While lying in a hospital bed looking out the window, I notice a beautiful array of flowers resting between two park benches.

I hear some of my family discussing whether or not "Shawn will ever get out of this coma." I hear my mom's voice as she says "be quiet he can hear you. Only speak positive around him"

"He needs to absorb positive energy from us", my dad added.

It was nice to hear my father supporting my mother in front of the family. It was nice to know their love had become genuine again. I did not know if I would ever see it again in my lifetime.

I am having difficulty trying to speak but can move my hands slowly towards the call button.

I press it.

Within seconds nurses come in and then the family. Mostly everybody is saying "Are you okay? Are you okay?"

I shake my head and smile as everybody stands crowded around me.

My niece Samantha says "look uncle I think he is here for you . . . everyone turns to see a beautiful raven walk on the windowsill.

I smile and visit with different friends and family members as they say: "only you could go through this without breaking any bones!"

There are two officers waiting outside to question me despite the nurse's clear and repeated indications of my need for rest.

I have asked all of my friends and family if they have heard from Cali and the slight hesitation before their answers make me feel uneasy. Most people just can't lie on cue without giving subtle messages.

Each of our bodies receives them every day. They may be subtle messages from the music repeatedly playing in our minds or stronger messages by the people we associate with. I learned this especially while being in the coma.

I remember feeling how nervous my sister was based upon her voice when she spoke.

I remember the certainness expressed in Joe Joe's voice. He always said "his uncle was strong"

These subtle messages are the reason why the earth's magnetism is losing its polarity. Our adult bodies are 70% water and water can be positively and negatively charged. The negative issues in our lives and our fears and jealousies are slowly taking over in this timeframe as humans live on earth.

All the headlines in the press are rallying the negative spirits up and the iron core of the earth is heating up.

Then; we are fueling the fires as a result of all of the gossip and complaints; throwing water on hot coals. We cannot forget the iron core's ability of bursting the earthy water mains and creating jet-like streams. The land was flooded .

The flood waters remain even though God created the rainbow and clearly stated that he would never again do such a thing to the earth.

He did not however state how the world was designed. We are human for a reason and God allowed the donkey on the Ark for a reason as well.

I believe our world's negative energy will eventually allow the heaven's gate to open up again. Funny thing tough; the negative energy does not have the ability to open heaven's gates up. Can any amount of darkness be added to a well-lit room filled with faith, hope, love, respect, honor, valor, and courage?

A candle, however, can pierce the darkness with a vast array of light.
Your word is a lamp to my feet and a light for my path. Psalm 119:05
It is an outcry from the people who believe in God that is the key to unlocking heaven's gates.

It is the children walking to the second floor for prayer in the morning indicating the raven's return.

We are human.

We are sponges.

We are all puppets on angel's silver streams.

I know this for a fact because I am alive first of all. I thank God everyday first thing in the morning.

I also have no broken bones or permanent scars but surprisingly I have remembrance of everything since the kick in the head.

I remember the kick in the balls too. I now realize the last two years of my life were being lived as if I was in a different type of a coma. Aimlessly listening to and acting on my natural desires.

The officers enter the room and begin their interrogation of me.

I am lying on my back in a hospital bed, encumbered by tubes, needles and a breathing apparatus. As I drift in and out of consciousness; I am repeatedly questioned about details of Cali's disappearance.

According to Mr. Mafia she has not returned from my house. She called and left a voicemail crying while she was with me. The phone call was made according to phone records at 10:35 P.M. Friday night.

I have a restraining order placed on me and I am not allowed within a certain distance from Mr. Mafia or Cali.

Life has certainly gone full-circle for me.

I think it to be far pleasanter sitting in the shade comfortably, rubbing crushed ghost pepper into my eyes than to go about in the sun hunting up evidence.

Thankfully the mob set-up is not going to work because I have five witnesses to say I was playing cards with them at 10:35 P.M.

My guess is Mr. Mafia is attempting to frame me now for Cali's disappearance.

I begin to explain the circumstances in detail to the interrogating officers. I begin with the details of the accident which occurred on Halloween night leading up to the assault which occurred in the bathroom of my house.

HALLOWEEN NIGHT:

It is 7:40 and I have no idea what my costume is going to be.

I hear my mom's voice on the answering machine, and she is concerned about the spiritual guides' message from the reading the other night at the church. I hear her say the words "Amber Alert Halloween Night."

The intercom pauses for a moment and then I hear Cali's voice . . . "Your gonna love my outfit. I will see ya soon. I am running at least 15 minutes late though!"

I am glad to have the extra fifteen minutes! I just popped a vicodin and I have already been drinking some Ed Hardy vodka. I purchased it in Vegas after having a very good night.

Cali is driving to the party; so, I am comfortable with getting my drink on early. My mind is working overtime while I grab my White Sox jersey. I decided to be the White-Sox all purpose player, Nick Swisher. Many people have told me I look a lot like him.

For the first time the written name on the back of the jersey meant a lot more to me while reading it. . . "Swisher"

I pause and take a deep breath. I see the remains of the necklace resting on the dresser which burst from the chest of Cali a couple of nights ago.

I begin to breathe more calmly. I remember reading II Timothy 1:7 "I have not given you the spirit of fear."

I close my eyes and begin to flip through my opened journal. After a deep exhalation, I open my eyes.

February 13, 2007 (10:06pm)

We attract what we think!

I know we have all heard the saying "You are what you think"; have we just said and heard the phrase so often the entire message has been lost. I am serious here. I have been questioning why it is that we have attracted certain things in our life.

We also continue to attract things, messages, loved ones, etc. If we are not paying attention to our own individual thoughts, we may have difficulty scrambling through the mundane activities of our life to better determine our destiny in life.

It is our chance each day as we rise to allow certain thoughts to enter into further thoughts. I myself have been struggling this year and my belief system in this world has truly been tested.

I now find myself as a very big piece to the puzzle without having noticed it and I have been trying to pay attention to my feelings as best as possible.

So, I have to ask; if I while paying attention to my relationships with others, truly paying attention to people while they speak as if I am playing cards. If I have had difficulty understanding my purpose in life; I can't imagine people trying to survive this world without having paid this much attention to detail at all.

The truth of the matter is this . . . all of us are and have been playing this game of life according to the rues of men (I meant to type rules but do not find it funny that rues was typed there). The pity of men has been the basis for how we are all living! It is this pity, this regret that has been the guidelines laid out to us since we were children.

Each generation has a new thought suggested to them and it is these series of thoughts that have led us down this pathway we are all on. This pathway was supposed to be definite until we have grown defiant to it. Our actions have led us to where we are and our actions will lead us where we are going to be. GV: "We are all sponge ornaments hanging from a tree."

GV: "The World is a Sponge." In parenthesis I read (He spoke to me clearly!) GV means God's Voice.

GV: "Even if you do not agree with 'my theory of the world you are living in.' It would be wise of you to entertain your own thoughts as you pass each day in your life." I realized everything has been happening for a reason for a long time. I just did not realize until this particular moment why God persisted, I continue to have this dragonstyle luck as some have called it.

My fear subsides entirely. I know something beyond strange is happening. Dreamality forms as I am in-fostered into a childhood memory. I see the clouds taking shape in the sky; forming the outline of my shoulders and the back of my head. I open my eyes and see this same image has formed itself across the computer screen. It is my shadow. It is me typing my book.

It is part of a "Pipe Dream" according to one of my best friends Dave.
"I think you have a better odds becoming an author than you do owning a casino in Vegas. " Dave says to me.

My fear is gone. I am present and I fully understand the importance of remaining in this wonderful feeling. The calmness is tranquil.

I decide to take another deep breath and open the journal to another random page. I happened to open it on page 22.

"Deuces Wild", the name of my imaginary casino, comes to mind. I begin to read:

"At a time when our lordly Masters in Great Britain will be satisfied with nothing less than the depreciation of American freedom, it seems highly necessary that something shou'd be done to avert the stroke and maintain the liberty which we have derived from our Ancestors; but the manner of doing it to answer the purpose effectually is the point in question.

The more I consider a Scheme of this sort, the more ardently I wish success to it, because I think there are private, as well as public advantages to result from it; the former certain, however precarious the other may prove; for in respect to the latter I have always thought that by virtue of the same power (for here alone the authority derives) . . . On the other hand, that the Colonies are considerably indebted to Great Britain, is a truth universally acknowledged. That many families are reduced, almost, if not quite, to penury and want, from the low ebb of their fortunes, and Estates daily selling for the discharge of Debts, the public papers furnish but too many melancholy proofs of. And that a scheme of this sort will contribute more effectually than any other I can devise to immerge the Country from the distress it at present labours under, I do most firmly believe, if it can be generally adopted. And I can see but one set of people (the Merchants excepted) who will not, or ought not, to wish well to the Scheme; and that is those who live genteelly and hospitably, on clear Estates. . . .

The quotation is dated April 5'th 1769. It is a letter from George Washington to George Mason. This letter was written before their friendship dissolved.

I can assure you right now I have no idea why any of this is happening. It reminds me of a book. A book I have not written yet.

I close the journal while sipping the remains of my glass.

My phone alert indicating an email has arrived sounds in the distance. . . "I am Rocky BalBosi"

A Harris bank representative has sent me an email after meeting with me earlier in the week. Her email reads "It was a pleasure to have met and spoke with you this morning. I am reading a book right now called "The Outliers". The more I thought about you; the more I thought about this book.

As I continue to get ready my "Pipe Dream" friend Dave calls me on the phone. "Hey Shawn remember I told you the strange occurrence of the woman who said she was going to send me a book in the mail. We'll she sent me a letter in the mail, and it says ' "Dave- it was a pleasure meeting you. I could not find the book I mentioned to you, but I decided to buy it for you instead…"

Shawn interrupts Dave and says "let me guess ..."

"What do you mean let me guess?" Dave says.

Shawn interjects-"The name of the book is 'The Outliers".

At this moment, it feels like life is interweaving pieces of a complex jig-saw puzzle together. The outcome is yet to be determined.

I am slightly scared.

It is Halloween.

Amber Alert!

Cali is here. Immediately I think she is a blessing. She is dressed as a little Indian Girl, and she looks hot. Her dark braids frame her face perfectly. The maroon hair ties are accented with hot pink lace ribbons. Cali spins-a smile on her face- adding more and more love to the room.

She speaks in her sexy Chinese voice. . ."Ah u wanta see more?" I can not move as she tugs her already hiked skirt up a little further. It is tan and looks like corduroy. Her knee-high boots match perfectly. Her fingers release the cupped bottom of her skirt and begin to circle the hot pink lace ribbons. She is watching herself in the mirror while she bends forward.

Her hand grips the only moving part of my body. "Luv u long time!" Cali says while bending completely forward. A bright pink border outlines her boy shorts. Her hand guides my body to the darkened area of her skin-colored boy shorts.

I do not remember the "forty plus minutes- we are now late" driving to the party. She moves me anyway she wants at times.

I look over at her face and legs while driving. She is even hotter because of the sex we just had. Her eyes close longer than I think to be safe while driving. She grabs my hand from under the steering wheel and places it on her gear shift.

We are all smiles walking up to the party. We are more than happy to be in love.

The sex is great and finally we have found the person of our mutual dreams. We have found a partner who wants to add to each one of our day's happiness.

Heads turn from every direction when we approach. The gentleman wearing the white shirt does not look happy to see Cali. He does not appear to be happy seeing me neither.

My spirit circles around his character practically making him dizzy while he speaks with Cali. He is memorized with how well she looks and agrees as Cali says "not to say anything to his best friend. His best friend is Mr. Mafia, and he is going to say he ran into me at the party, but I was with a group not an individual like that guy!" he nodded his head in my direction.

I see another guy make a phone call. He looks directly at me. He nods his head a couple times while saying yes.

I wanted to yell out "how ridiculous obvious all of this was… "

I freeze . . . realizing exactly how obvious they are making it.

Cali comes running over and says, "Let's go inside Shawn!" My hands squeezed her hands and she squeezes back even harder. Cali does not scare easily.

Less than a half hour later my spoken words are easily understood. "Cali, we have to get out of here! This room is the worst place we should be in!

Those are the same two guys who seemingly have been following us since we got here. They are the only Mexicans at the party and they do not seem to be conversing with anyone."

Cali jumps up, aggressively yanks my hand like I am a prisoner of some sort and pulls me up the stairs. We run frantically through the kitchen and out the patio doors. Her jump off the two-story deck is cushioned by the hot tub cover below. I am sure my added weight is going to send me through the cover especially because Cali already landed on it. I am surprised by it and Cali's strength. She just climbed a 6' wood fence faster than my neighbor's angry cat; faster than a ring tailed lemur.

The hot tub cover is solid when my body smacks against it.
On top of the hill awaits three pine trees. I immediately begin to think of those pine trees. The same pine trees I saw on the way home from the gym.

There are two guys standing on the sidewalk looking in all directions. One of them appears to be on his phone.

We are shaking. We are cold. It is dark. We are scared.

Cali and I lay in each other's arms. Hearts pumping; we begin to kiss for the first time with our eyes open. The two guys walk further away from our vehicle. Our kisses last just long enough to settle our nerves a bit.

We are scrambling towards the back of another house and out of sight from our pursuers. It's amazing how close the two of us remain to each other.

The temperature is dropping. Our clothing, especially Cali's, is not sufficient. The Durango, registered in Mr. Mafia's name, is still a good distance away from us.

Cali begins to run quickly towards the vehicle and her head start is not sufficient enough for me. I open the backdoor to the Durango and Cali jumps under the heavy blanket. The backseats were already folded down and the cold heavy blanket provides warmth to both of us.

We are shaking. We are cold. It is dark. We are scared.

"Shawn- let's just stay here for a while… I am not sure where they are, and they will recognize the car if we drive past them!" Cali's words pierce the stillness.

My body feels like I am camping. There is no flat surface anywhere underneath me.

I think I already know the answer to the question I am about to ask. I have to ask anyway. "Cali- what exactly are we laying on back here?"

"They are my stuffed animals. I just cleared out my mom and dad's house!" Cali responds.

One by one I lift the stuffed animals from underneath me. I continue to lift them while saying "we have to . . . (my hands and words are shaking as I pick up the fifth stuffed animal) "leave now!"

We need to drive! Drive! Drive!" Shawn states with urgency.

"Is anyone following us?" Cali slurs from under the blanket.

My mind is more attentive to the streets than her question. I am thankful for the first time in awhile for being a business owner. The familiarity of the streets would not be recognizable if it weren't for the constant estimates I go on in this area.

The irony makes me laugh for a moment. Cali screams "Is anyone following us?" By the time Cali's words stop echoing off the Durango's steamed windows she is on her knees looking out the back window.

Stuffed animals are being thrown about the backseat and Cali begins repeating something out loud faster and faster. She removes her jacket first then her shirt.

In the rear-view mirror, I see her braids dangling down across her bra. She tells me she is getting hot and sick to her stomach.

She begs for us to pull over.

My grade school buddy Stan used to live in the Joliet area we are now approaching so I am very familiar with this "not so good- side of town". We make a quick turn down a one-way street while Cali is pleading for us to pull over.

We are approaching a white van parked on the side of the road.

Cali's vomit interrupts my thoughts and her words as she screams "pull over Shawn!"

We pull over and park quickly on an angle in front of a parked white van.

I race around to the passenger side back door and Cali is laying ¼ of the way out of the door. Face down, ass up. I grab both of her braids with each of my hands and step back to make sure my shoes were not being destroyed from the spewage on the street.

I do not remember what I noticed first- the loud crash or Cali's braids slipping out of my clenched hands. She drifted away from me as if she was caught in an under-toe. The Durango came to rest seventy-five feet away from me and up to the right side of the street.

I feel extreme heat on my entire body and begin to wonder if I am bleeding or on fire. I see no movement within the Durango since it came to a stop.

I see the white van still rolling up and over the curb. It came to rest on the front lawn approximately 100 feet from where it had been parked on the opposite side of the road. I turn slightly only to see the darkest of dark images I could picture on Halloween night. My vision is blurred slightly. Liquid darkness moves towards me. The smoke is escaping from the smashed chrome grill of the demolished Escalade which has abruptly stopped two feet from my chest.

I see two people flailing their arms inside. My eyes meet with the driver of the Escalade. It is the Mexican guy from the party.

The Escalade had slammed into the parked van behind us.
I do not know what to think. I cannot hear much of anything besides this ringing in my ears. I begin to run towards the Durango more concerned and scared right now.

I can see Cali wedged between the folded down seats. There are stuffed animals all over the street.

"Cali, are you okay?
Can I move you? "Shawn asks.

"Shawn Shawn- what happened? Is it them? Did they come after us?" Cali slithers into my arms while asking her questions. "

Cali, yeah it is them let me carry you!" Shawn says. I carry Cali around the apartment building and place her in a dark corner. I immediately run to the Durango and grab a blanket.

As I race back in the direction of the dark corner, I notice Cali is shaking back and forth. She is drunk, cold, and entering into shock. I wrap her frail body in the blanket.

She is non-responsive to my question and my statements:

"Cali, I need your phone!"

"Can I have your phone?"

"I do not know where mine is and I have to call someone to come and get us out of here!"

I run back to her Durango and see the two Mexican guys jumping into another black vehicle. It is a black newer style suburban with twenty-inch rims on squealing tires.

A tow truck pulls up while I rifle through Cali's purse.

Two overweight Mexican women get out of the suburban and quickly change places with the two Mexican men from the party.

My mom's phone is ringing. Even at thirty-five years old she is the first person I think of calling. This location is close to her church.

My mom answers the phone "Are you okay Shawn?"

"Yes, mom but I need you to come here. I was in an accident near your church."

The tow truck driver was already pulling the Escalade out of the way!

I race back over to the secluded corner between the buildings and Cali leans into me and whispers into my ear "well now we know what Amber Alert Halloween Night meant."

"Hey there, hey there, put the phone down. I said put the phone down! An officer begins yelling. "

I am on the phone with my mom, and I am letting her know where I am- so she can come and get me!" Shawn harps back

"I don't care who you are on the phone with . . ." Officer friendly again. "Mom, by the way I am okay, but I have to put the phone ...

My mom interrupts my sentence "Yeah-I hear him Shawn. I will call you back on this number when I get ..."

The officer closes the flip-phone.

I try desperately to explain to these officers what just happened, but they are too busy running back and forth trying to find discrepancies in Cali and my story.

I hear Cali raise her voice to the officers – "You guys are supposed to protect and serve and you guys are trying to intimidate me. I am hurt and your concern should start there. We were chased tonight by friends of my ex-boyfriend who is heavily involved in the mafia."

For as long as I live; I will never forget the officers' response to her drunken frank honesty: "Does your new boyfriend know you are driving a vehicle registered to your ex-boyfriend?" A perfect question at an optimal time.

Another younger officer intervenes the groups discussion and says "those Mexican girls are making no sense… they claim to be driving the vehicle and their stories are conflicting. Plus, the tow truck driver was here trying to pull the Escalade away from the scene before any of us got here."

Shawn interjects "You see; I told you guys. You're too busy over here thinking Cali and my story is far-fetched but it is the truth. Those girls were not driving the Escalade. I saw the drivers jump into a black suburban. Those tire tracks right there were left from it as it squealed away. Cali's ex boyfriend, Mr. Mafia, came after the two of us tonight!"

The officers look at each other; only some of them half-surprised.

Cali's phone rings. I answer it. It is my mom.

"Shawn, Shawn is everything okay? I am here. There are cops everywhere!" I immediately think of Cali because she calls me Shawn Shawn. I look at Cali and can not believe what we have just experienced.

"Yes Mom, everything is okay. Give me a second please they are placing Cali into the ambulance."

I thought of her eyes the other night right before we listened to the spiritual healers. We call it the "Dunkin Doughnut Stare".

The peace was surreal then.

The anxiety is real now.

The ambulance drives off.

The grill from the white van lies on the street next to the curb surrounded by stuffed animals. I bend down, take a much-needed deep breath and notice my sunglasses hanging on the grill from the white van. I purchased those sunglasses in San Diego two years ago.

In my opinion Halloween night was Mr. Mafia's first attempt at taking our lives. My guess is he made her stage a phone call at 10:30 P.M. and then forced her to come here and kick me in the nuts so I would have to restrain her in some way. She listened to him and figured she would come here and no matter what she did to me she did not think I would ever "attack her".

I was scared. I had no idea what was happening. She was the one who called me, and it was 12:30 A.M. when she called. She took a taxi to my house.

She wanted to see me and then within minutes after she arrives, she is outraged and kicking me in the balls.

Now I clearly understand why she was calling me a "dumbfuck". I had fallen for his trap.

I was later arrested for the murder of Cali- a woman I truly loved. The reason why I believe Mr. Mafia's plan worked is because I claim to have seen Cali on Saturday morning and called a cab for her around 2:30 P.M. Her time of death was reported to be at least 15 hours before between 11:00 P.M.-1:30 A.M.

Her time of death could have occurred within minutes after I was dropped off at my home. Traces of blood are found on the outside of my house matching Cali's blood type.

I did just over two years in the prison in my mind and something broke free for me in the case while I was behind these bars.

The raven returned.

A key witness has been placed in the witness protection program. He hid in the forest while Mr. Mafia heavily assaulting Cali. He testifies to having seen her body being dumped in a river near her apartment at 11:15 P.M.

Her body is found the next day and I am given a full pardon. While packing my belongings in a small "Solid Run Cubox" I notice the first picture I saw after having come out of the coma. It is an angel holding a wishbone. Her wing seems to be broken.

Cali did not truly come to see me the night after playing cards. There has never been any record of any taxi service dropping her off or picking her up. Her life was taken while I was playing cards at 11:15.

After over two years in prison, I am finally set free. I realize there to be only one rational explanation:

Mr. Mafia staged the call from Cali to himself at 10:30 P.M. 45 minutes later he was dropping her body in the river near her apartment- the eyewitness was sure of the time. It was 11:15 P.M.

It enabled him the time to drive to my house and leave me for death less than an hour later.

During the time I lay in the pool of blood I received cellular calls from Cali. She visits my house via taxicab.

She is upset. We fight.

She comes here to see if she really loves me.

She does.

Believing is seeing as the angel flaps and adjusts her left wing. She begins by saying "They are no different than you and me!"

I picture the wings of the angel folded-up underneath her back while my hand grasps her throat.

The un-hung mirrored painting lay broken on the closet floor.

Her skin sliced three times just above her left wrist. The wounds heal quickly while she pulls the broken pieces of mirror from her flesh.

In her life of mirrors, she visited me after her death. She flaps and adjusts her left wing. She kicked me in the balls…she changed my life forever!

The conversations I have with God while being in the coma are amazing. He and a group of angels explain to me "how the feelers line up with the keys" and I see the earth's tectonic plates shifting and rotating in a variety of fashions.

I see numerous retention ponds man has created in front of many subdivisions throughout the U.S.

I see great floods and famine spread throughout the U.S.

I see attorneys as captains of many of the ships.

I see businesses and banks going bankrupt.

I see an Olympic athlete smoking a bong.

I see professional baseball players using steroids to "enhance their games".

I see the wealthy foolishly spending their bonuses and bail-out money.

I see a famous quarterback being arrested for having "dog fights" and another one sending pictures of his penis to an attractive woman.

I see Britney and other famous singers being involved in custody battles and physical assaults.

I see the parent's of different children tackling and throwing punches at coaches and referees.

I see Dennis Rodman on Celebrity Apprentice.

I see the same things everybody in this world has seen. Accept I see them as highlight reel one after another. At the end of the highlight reel, I see myself on the phone with my uncle telling him "I want to be a made guy."

I see Osama Bin Laden in the Los Angeles airport December 23'rd 2008.

I see myself on my knees asking, "why have you forsaken me?"

I see myself falling to my knees after having been hit by the baseball bat.

I see Jesus laughing in a good way and in this case seeing is believing.

I believe God gave us different tongues to unite the human race when the world needs it most. I am sure many of you agree the world needs it most right now.

I really do hope each of us as individuals realize there is a lot more to life than just walking through it aimlessly.

We are spirits. Our souls are searching.

We are all "made" men and women.

We are "made" by God.

I hope everyone begins to pursue their Pipe Dreams more.

That is what we are "made" for.

We are made to trust.

We are made to love our neighbors as ourselves. We have been given many great examples along the way too.

Prior to coming out of the coma . . . Jesus, a group of angels, Noah and Nuwa all continued to repeat the words Galatians 5:16 to me:

"So, I say, live by the Spirit, and you will not gratify the desires of the sinful nature. For the sinful nature desires what is contrary to the Spirit, and the Spirit what is contrary to the sinful nature. They are in conflict with each other, so that you do not do what you want. But if you are led by the Spirit, you are not under law. The acts of the sinful nature are obvious: sexual immorality, impurity, and debauchery; idolatry and witchcraft; hatred, discord, jealousy, fits of rage, selfish ambition, dissensions, factions, and envy; drunkenness, orgies and the like. I warn you, as I did before, that those who live like this will not inherit the kingdom of God. But the fruit of the Spirit is love, joy, peace, patience, kindness, goodness, faithfulness, gentleness, and self-control. Against such things there is no law. Those who belong to Jesus have crucified the sinful nature with its passions and desires. Since we live by the Spirit, let us keep in step with the Spirit."

I press the call button.

I await the world's response as I cast myself into the waters- I've been bottled up too long.

I've been acting out of fear instead of love. I believe many of us are and have.

The earthquake shook the Midwest while Zissafiss and Jesus dribbled a basketball between their legs speaking these words to me "You will see more clearly if you follow me."

I only know of one human being who has walked on water, so I think listening to his advice is important.

California is constantly rumbling for a reason- the world is a big sponge.

The rues of men seem to be the Goliath.

"Dreamality" is my slingshot.

My spirit begins to tell me in a happy and proud voice, "All the angels are present, all of us are proud to be here with you!

You have our blessing. So run quickly through this world, remain faithful to your promises to yourself, and above all else. Never Cease! Believing and Seeing Always!" Afterthought:

I recall receiving an email from an editor while sitting at a baseball game with my parents. In the email, the second version of my book is politely turned down. I remember stating in my response email that "I just so happened to be sitting at a White Sox game and believe in three strikes." I had two on me already.

That night I purchased the Nick Swisher t-shirt I was wearing on Halloween night. Is it as simple as z and s? I asked myself?

"Swishhh! Swishhh!, Swissssh!"-the sound loudest right before the necklace blew away from Cali's chest.

The government secret her boyfriend shared with her prior to hanging himself was shared with me. It could help change America.

I pick up my phone and decide to send a text trying to explain the constant rumbling in California:

"Osama B in L.A. den"

CHAPTER XIV

PAY ATTENTION TO DETAILS

I have searched

within

these words I find . . . neither one of us can go back in time.
Structuring the father and son relationship occurred a long time ago.
But I will paddle unlike ever before until you know.
Sitting at the kitchen table nearly five years have came and went
recalling the words you said while staring at a successful blueprint.
"Pay attention to the details; the details . . .
make the drawing!"
Elevated before my eyes,
the second level of my life, has been made clear
the spiral staircase of your words suddenly adhere.
I know you have seen the staircase with no central support;
33 steps compared to that of the life of the Lord.
your time spent remodeling

> *crafting wood*
>
> *with all that you know . . .*
>
> *I ask how does it stand; how do I stand*
>
> *I ask you; do you understand*
>
> *these words;*
>
> *Pay attention to the details" ?*
>
> *They make the drawing of life:*
>
> *Your relationships,*
>
> *Your sons,*
>
> *Your daughter,*
>
> *Your wife.*
>
> *This is one of the thirty three steps.*
>
> *Floating for as long as it has--as we have !*

Traveling during the holidays is typically quite entertaining to say the least but imagine my surprise when my eyes lifted to meet what appeared to be the eyes of Osama Bin Laden at the San Diego airport. At the time he appeared to be approx 51 years old, well dressed comfortably in jogging like clothing material but expensive for sure. He had a very manicured look to him; even his 10-12" beard came directly to a point. He certainly seemed a bit uncomfortable as my eyes were studying him and the associates who were momentarily next to him.

I thought to myself; no, it can't be!

Convinced my experience with Cali was certain to be adding to my already heightened imagination, I decided not to follow him at all and sat down for some lunch before the flight back home.

After gracefully landing in Chicago, I found myself entering the bedroom to unpack while listening to the television. That's when the haze returned just as strong as previously described in this story. I expected one of my friends to be standing in front of me within seconds when the news reports began to alert on the television channels; one after the next. "Harbor Drive Closed Due to Suspicious Object!"

San Diego Police say the 2700 block of Harbor Drive near Lindbergh Field has been closed both northbound and southbound as they investigate a report of a suspicious package outside the Coast Guard station.

The package was discovered about 12:30 P.M. and the Coast Guard secured its base. The package was found near the main gate by security personnel, Coast Guard Officials said.

San Diego Harbor Police have established a perimeter around the suspicious package. The San Diego Fire-Rescue Department ordinance disposal unit also is on the scene.

San Diego police officer Jim Johnson says the Harbor Drive is closed to traffic in both directions between West Laurel Street and the airport rental car lots.

Holiday travelers trying to reach the airport should drive from the Point Loma direction. "

The word suspicious began echoing around the walls of my room. The s becomes a z and pretty soon the z becomes a s.

"Suspicious!", "Suspicious!", "Suspicious!"

My ears were in need of being covered due to the excessive ringing until the haze escaped the room as if it wasn't supposed to be there and someone was coming.

I certainly did not consider this to be a spiritual orgasm because the feeling during and after felt entirely different. This was a definitely a warning or at least a shocking verification of what I had seen earlier in the day in San Diego. At the moment- I did not know how else to interpret it but was thankful there was only a buzz now left ringing in my ear.

Once my body was capable of moving, I immediately call the San Diego Police Department. The officer asks me how tall the man I saw and thought to be Osama Bin Laden was and I answered him by saying 6' or so. Then the officer immediately replied saying "Thanks for the call but the real Bin Laden is 6'4" so there's no way this person could have been him!"

His voice seemingly further from the phone as the last part of his sentence I can barely hear. He hangs up abruptly .

Immediately, I start to think Bin Laden walked around on stilts or had ways of creating a physical description on camera appear much different than reality.

However, I knew there was nothing more I could do at the time besides making proper notes and details of the events I was experiencing. The entire topic brought back many difficult and disturbing memories, so I began saying the Lord's Prayer and embolism.

"Our Father- Who art in Heaven.

Hallowed be thy Name.

Thy Kingdom come

Thy will be done,

on earth as it is in Heaven.

Give us this day our daily bread

and forgive us our trespasses,

as we forgive those who trespass against us.

And lead us not into temptation,

 but deliver us from evil.

Deliver us, Lord, from every evil, and grant us peace in our day.

In your mercy keep us free from sin and protect us from all anxiety.

As we wait in joyful hope for the coming of our Savior Jesus Christ our Lord.

Amen!"

The haze returns differently in color this time and with a fragrance from beyond this world. Peace overtakes the room completely as the hues of pink, yellow and orange move in the direction of my laptop.

It is easy to remember the details of this experience after saying this particular prayer because my laptop turned on by itself for the first time. The haze of colors swirled like a mini waterspout approximately 5' 8" tall and the exact length and width of the Dell Latitude E6540 which is 15"x10". It was as if the haze was swirling into the laptop and it begins disappearing into it while seemingly powering it on.

Mind you, I did say "first time", so I am hesitant to move towards it right away and actually waiting for it to physically open up and or explode.

Nothing happens for a minute or two, so I swiftly move in its direction to open it!

Thinking of these words to say

This song my voice as I pray.

I stand outside; outside my window

A breath from God moves the shadows;

an unchanging breeze accepted by the leaves

fallen to my knees.

Memories locked inside a vault I cannot see;

These tears are in my eyes

The storm of all this pain

I'm calling out your name

Asking you . . . to rescue . . . me

from the pain, I hide from friends,

a pain that never ends.

These thorns surround what I say . . .

in everything I do

let my heart and its ways . . .

surround you.

Sinking in the words I heard

My heart (becomes) just a traveler.

I walk around; around the falsehood

there has to be some good.

I lay quietly on this bed of leaves,

fall peacefully asleep

into dreams locked inside

an anchor that weighs me.

These thoughts are in my mind

The storm while I'm out at sea

drowning away the times

Asking you . . . to rescue . . . me!

Burning with the fire in dismay

this house, my boat castaway

near an island; frozen in summer . . .

times they suddenly begin to blur

many people say - " we might see better times "

But what I'm . . . .

saying, this song my voice

a breath I know you prime.

I'm left without a choice

my breath can put out this . . . . . . .blaze.

Calling out your name

Asking you . . . . to rescue . . . .

This is actually when things initially start to become even more bizarre. Words began coming to my mind so quickly and with so much intention and meaning I could not type fast enough. I immediately grab my mini voice recorder and start repeating everything I hear as if I'm an interpreter of the same language.

The laptop and myself start floating in the center of space which could be anywhere actually and since my mind is literally in space while it's happening; everything is a part of everything in this galaxy.

While floating, I'm continuing to see the randomness of chaos begin to make perfect sense. I'm just now realizing I can use my hands to draw in the air exactly what

I'm thinking.

It is a very cool feeling watching it appear in front of me and indicating some sort of time travel is occurring at this point. Apparently, I have just traveled into the end of this meta-verse; it is as if I have flown into a bubble which graciously brings me back to the initial point of impact after absorbing me.

I'm giving the option to return to land or to continue in space by drawing an arrow in front of me towards the direction I want to go.

I immediately enter another galaxy of space and can visit any planet without issue. Even the stars can be touched without causing me harm.

Suddenly my body awakens on the top of a heated mountain. It looks like a one-of-a-kind waterfall rainforest and my body moves by levitating in the direction it needs to go. There are all types of beautiful animals here; some of which have not been discovered yet; but all of them are smiling at me as I pass them by.

I am levitating towards what appears to be a swing rope in front of the waterfall. A hot air balloon floats over the cove just out in front of it. I grab onto the swing rope which brings me in and out of the waterfall. All of a sudden lava begins replacing the water beneath me and I notice the rope in the sky starting to smoke and it quickly catches fire.

There's steam creating a haze similar to the one I'm used to seeing directly in front of the basket of the hot air balloon.

Just as the swinging rope burns thru; my Tarzan like body goes hurling thru the air. The steamy haze moves into position of the burner just as the rope disappears into the lava beneath it. The hot air balloon powered by the haze bursts into the atmosphere with me in it thankfully.

I barely have any time to gather my thoughts as the ringing of a phone is heard among the literal mist of the waterfall and lava clashing beneath me. I look down at the ringing phone and it is an Iridium Extreme in Sporting Camo. It's definitely fitting for me to be answering my first Sat phone during the experience.

"Hello...is this, Shawn Bosi ?" The woman on the other end of the line speaks anxiously.

"Yes, This is him." Shawn Responds.

"OMG, I am so glad I was given this number to get a hold of you. This is Jessica! We met on the Grand Opening night at The Stingaree in downtown San Diego. I recall you saying your cousin Vince was one of the top bounty hunters in the nation and that he lived in San Diego like me. Do you remember me and the conversation?"

"Holy Sheeet Jessica... the Grand Opening of the Stingaree was the hottest spot in the Gaslamp Quarter; I definitely remember. (most of the night) We met across the catwalk right by the piano at the invite only private party. How have you been?" Shawn asks.

"Yes- that's me. I'm great and terrible all at the same time and I need you help if possible. I got a great job offer on Hawaii and want to bring my two dogs. I have papers for both of them, but my boyfriend will not give them back to me because he is pissed, I'm leaving him. If there's any way your cousin can help, please let me know! " Jessica yells.

"I'll call him now, Jessica" Shawn says.

"Hey, before I let you go... I'm sure you saw all the Ferraris and Lambos parked by the curb next to the red-carpet sidewalks where the hostess sign in tables were the Grand Opening Night right? " Shawn Asks.

"OMG Yes. Stingaree was advertising their grand opening for months on the radio. I don't know if you remember but I remember telling you how impressed I was; a Chicago Guy- somehow got an invite to the biggest grand opening in San Diego in years and also had VIP access across the catwalk!" Jessica states excitedly. "yes, yes exactly the reason why I brought it up. Just to be 100% straight forward going forward; I bullshitted my way in with my brother and two other friends that night. I had no invitation to the event. Further, I bet my friends I could get in the VIP party and won otherwise I would have never met you!" Shawn explains with much laughter.

" Don't worry about getting your dogs back; Vince and I are very close. Consider it done!' Shawn says with confidence while hanging up the phone.

Fast forward thru the back and forth Sat phone calls between the parties involved while floating in the hot air balloon which the spiritual haze is powering.

Vince is provided with a park location along with certain days and hours normally frequented.

Two attempts later for Vince is all it took. Let's just say when an average guy is surrounded at a dog park by multiple Bounty Hunters who are holding copies of the dogs' papers in their hands stating Jessica as their legal owners . . . pretty soon those same Bounty Hunters were holding Jessica's dogs which then led to Jessica holding them both.

I must have dozed off in mid flight because I find myself waking to a voice message on the Sat phone from Jessica saying: "Shawn; I got the dogs back today from Vince and will be flying to Hawaii in a few weeks. You will love the place I am watching on Maui and are welcome to stay anytime this winter. Please make your way across the pond! Mahalo! "

CHAPTER XV

THE HAWAII WINTER GATEWAY (S)

For this portion of the book, I have to go backwards a bit in order to go forwards. Just like in business, after having a year or two years of expansion; it's always best to have a year or two of contraction. This method typical ends up helping stabilize the growth and I'm hoping the same applies to book writing and becoming a National Best-Selling Author; so here it goes .

As stated previously Harris Bank approves a signature loan in the amount of $50,000.00 while stating " This was one of the easiest loans they ever wrote!" The loan officer was encouraging about expanding my business while pursuing my career as an author.

The " I Can Do It!" 2006 writer's conference in Vegas had a supreme line up of authors. I saw and met Doreen Virtue, Gregg Braden, Dr. Masaru Emoto, Lisa Williams, and Steven Farmer.

Immediately after the conference I began thinking about next year's conference and learned my favorite author, Dan Millman, was going to be on Maui.

Chapter One referenced "It's a Sign" and Page 22 of this original manuscript referenced the serendipitous coincidences with respect to Dan Millman and the gas station etc. but God's Pace was becoming more adherent throughout all of these occurrences. The galaxy tour was the first indication of the randomness of chaos making perfect sense.

The newspaper reporter for The Maui Weekly covering the 2007 Writer's Conference was on assignment interviewing some of the attendees of the event.

We immediately connect during one of the presentations. Our continual glances at one another creates difficulties in note taking for me at least. She reminds me of Gloria Estefan so hopefully that better helps you understand the difficulty in note taking reference better. She asked me to lunch and I was trying not to be pushy after she said the story she was writing was supposed to be based on the locals attending the event. Gloria wasn't sure if "I could be included in her piece."

Shawn smiled saying "I traveled a great length to attend this event so that's noteworthy!"

Gloria responded with " you don't have to convince me Shawn! I will have to persuade my editor to include a non local author's story as part of the piece; in order to get your name in the article."

Gloria must have been good at convincing because Shawn's name was in The Maui Weekly, referencing his book originally titled " God's Pace ".

Seeing it was icing on the cake for me. It made me real (eyes) how unique the experience was and I feel even more blessed. At one point during the conference I was walking to one of the ballrooms to see Dan Millman's presentation. I was turning the corner and first saw the greeter by the door while almost bumping into Dan himself who was also walking in the door at the same time from the opposite direction and corner.

The greeter says "Hey Dan! Nice to see you. What are you doing here?" Dan answers " Hey there! Nice to see you as well... I am presenting here ." Immediately I begin chiming into their conversation saying- " and since Dan is my favorite author- I'm here to see his presentation!"

The greeter gave us both a very perplexing look and said " But Dan you don't present at this ballroom tonight!" leaving us both considerably confused for the moment.

As God's Pace would have it; both myself and Dan Millman were going to the same presentation, at the same exact time, at an entirely different ballroom from where the event was actually being held.

We begin walking through the hallways to the correct ballroom together. These minutes spent together at The Wailea Beach Marriott Resort & Spa on Maui with the beautiful oceanic backdrop is breathtaking.

The comfortable haze accompanies us as well. I first realize its' presence stepping on the elevator. The experience truly allows my dream of becoming an author much more tangible. The minutes feel like hours during our conversation while walking.

I'm holding the door for him at the correct ballroom as he says " we are fashionably late together Shawn. Glad to have met and will talk more throughout the conference. Don't forget authors are human just like you. "

The remaining three days of the conference the haze is with me. Throughout the presentations, while swimming and even while getting to know Gloria better. I am certainly glad to have three more full days to explore Maui now since the conference has ended.

Politely Gloria asks Shawn "If you're interested in a guided and private tour around Maui; I can go in for a couple hours in the morning and can be available to pick you up for a late brunch. I may even be able to expense it! If I get the go ahead to include you in the article from my editor, it's on me!"

This is one of those times where an obvious no brainer response is warranted from Shawn but as an aspiring author, I think he had to pause slightly before saying an offensive expletive followed by "YEAH".

While saying it to Gloria over the phone he immediately thought of the comedian Ron White and his "Dr. Phil Yacht Skit". He is certain as to how and why his brain compartmentalizes the response he just said to hear.

Thankfully she does not find the response offensive and expresses happiness to see Shawn tomorrow.

It's a calm night here. The warm sand under my toes reminds me of the heated floor in my bathroom. The sun is less than thirty minutes from setting and the only sound heard is the onset of a new beginning. I like to float in the Ocean as it sets and am preparing to enter the water while beginning to pray.

The heartbeat of these words written are to whoever is listening. The vibration of these words are obviously heard by Zissafiss because he appears in the ocean directly in front of me. There is no rational explanation as to how Shawn is capable of interpreting the whistles, clicks, squeaks, moans, grunts, trills, and creaking door sounds besides the haze continually being in his presence.

The mini recording device has limits and unfortunately it is left on the towel with his shirt, shades, and sandals. Excitedly he runs into the ocean. The attendee wrist band from the writing agents event still on his wrist.

Zissafiss' whistling becomes more and more intense. Celebratory for sure as he nods at Shawn's wrist with his nose while whistling. Real (Eyes) meeting Real (Eyes).

Zissafiss begins looking over at Shawn's towel and more intent fully at the mini recorder, shades, and sandals.

Zissafiss' whistling becomes more and more intense. Celebratory for sure as he nods at Shawn's wrist with his nose while whistling.

And the S becomes a Z and pretty soon the Z becomes an $.

Zissafiss' whistle blowing becomes a click. Click after Click after Click as the echolocation senses his and my surroundings.

Click after Click; multiple clicks is all I remember hearing for quite some time while the S changed into a dollar sign in between the Z and it.

Somehow the galaxy writing in the air was occurring while Zissafiss continued to make clicks, squeaks, moans, grunts, trills, and creaking door sounds.

The louder his whistle blows the more and more dollar signs are appearing in the galaxy sky. Click after Click and the S becomes a Z and pretty soon the Z becomes an $.

Zissafiss disappeared as fast as he appeared, but his whistling continues to be blowing and continues to resonate in Shawn's ears. While attempting to fall asleep at night; he is trying not to think about the entire experience including Gloria or Zissafiss.

Needless to say, there is not much sleep this night.
Shawn arises vibrant with a new hitch in his step. He's looking forward to Longhi's in South Kihei and his meeting with Gloria (pre-covid era).

The Road to Hana with her and the entire day is pretty much a blur after eating the artichoke hearts. The flourishing rainforests surround 620 curves and 59 bridges. There are stops along the way with views of dramatic seascapes, over 15 flowing waterfalls and plunging pools.

Some of the waterfalls require a bit of hiking to get to but Gloria knows this island inside and out, making this afternoon travel day more of a dreamlike reality.

The haze has pretty much taken over his actions as he is guided to wonderful meetings and experiences while Gloria navigates some of the challenging turns and narrow bridges along the way. The ensuing days all begin blending in for him afterwards.

The following day is round one of the swinging rope magical waterfall for Shawn. While levitating down to a private cove where only the brides and their bridesmaids would go prior to the marriages; Gloria begins to speak, " No men were ever welcome at the time according to the ancestry. No man knew of it because . . .

The sound of these next words is absorbed in the flower petals; 'No woman ever told.'

" The haze is guiding him, so he does his best listening and staying in the moment. I am considering selling my company. The brokerage firm initially said close to a million buyout.

However, I have been responsible for approx 1 million in estimates or jobs in motion already within the last 7-10 days. Actually it might be 5 days. Not while I'm on vacation but fifteen years into the future.

Figures don't add up but he certainly mentions it to Gloria at the time with potential hopes of actually selling it and moving to Hawaii. Little did he know there were Two Roads to Hana. He instantly merges with the galaxy balloon passing over the land the following winter.

Gloria and Shawn are somewhere in the mist of the one month they are spending together at Gloria's apartment.

They communicated often enough throughout the year and both have interest to better get to know one another. At this glance over balloon stage; I believe he has already met Gloria's father and brother now on two occasions over the span of 4 different events.

Her father is an author, business owner and healer! His magnetic sessions were of high interests to many locals and celebrities.

He told Oprah's booking rep "if Oprah wants a session, she will need to come in to see him. He was told "Oprah doesn't go to see anyone!"

Most Hawaiians and locals said " they never saw anyone buy so much patron for people they did not know; especially on Hawaii!" They were referencing Shawn and Gloria's night out with her brother. Many Alohas!

Gloria's father, however, sees many fractures of energy spirits feeding off of Shawn. He knows of his past injuries without touching him while he is fully clothed in this magnetic healing tent.

Her father's hands were as close to 1" off Shawn's body as he saw what he saw and does what he does. Shawn is told these spirits most often attach during negative experiences. Drinking excessive amounts of alcohol opens these fractures even more and the body becomes more receptive to negative energy spirits attaching.

Seizing the Moment like Horace in 23 BCE.

Needless to say, Shawn is all for this healing session and his body feels amazing as different hazes exit and different ones come in. The positive angels eliminating the leeches. Darker colors are replaced with positive high energy colors.

They are seemingly on different wavelengths during this trip exploring the island together. The green sand beach, winding roads, waterfalls, private coves, and black sand beach all take Shawn's mind to another place; yet it is the same place she is born and raised.

Her mind is taking her towards their future together more and more while he is staying in the moment as best as he can, completely guided by the haze and her.

The positive high energy colors continue to remain with Shawn and Gloria for much of this winter month of January 2009. Along the way; they both realize their hearts are in different places. Shawn is packing to leave after his one month stay as the positive high energy colors begin vibrating more and more.

The haze begins to steam up as much as it did in my bathroom earlier in the book. The waterspout like colors begin twirling in front of me as if I'm looking at a mirrored reflection of myself in a swirling blend of colors. This experience feels more like a sandstorm and in the distance I hear a slightly familiar ringtone. In a further distance; I hear the sounds of Zissafiss' whistles and clicks.

The Iridium Extreme in Sporting Camo Sat phone merges with my hand as I'm being dropped off at a rental car company in South Kihei approximately 25 minutes from the Maui airport. The winds are certainly howling.

On the other end of the line is the rental car owner saying he is 5 minutes away. It's one full calendar year later!!! After getting off the phone with him I call Jessica and she answers almost immediately. She is happy I have landed safely. She warns me of the storm coming and says, "although I'm excited to see you and show you this place; you may want to wait until tomorrow to make the drive!".

We are having difficulty hearing one another because I'm standing in a wind tunnel as I see the owner pulling into the lot.

Shawn says "Jessica; I appreciate the heads up but I'm not a fan of trying to find last minute arrangements especially on Maui. I'll message you once I see how the weather is along the drive though. Of course; I'm excited to see you too!",

They do not have the jeep rental available at the time but they do have a beautiful stick shift silver Audi available. The rental assistant says "if you do not like it; you can always bring it back and swap it out when a jeep becomes available."

Shawn says " I'm hoping to enjoy it because I'm going to the other side of the island with it tonight and it's a pretty good distance to bring it back."

The attendance face lost all expression and urgently responds with " You're going to the other side of the island tonight? If so; you better get a move on it because there's a terrible storm coming! That's why these winds are as bad as they are!"

Shawn says "The pilot briefly made an announcement about it because of the turbulence we were feeling near the end of the flight especially. I haven't quite felt turbulence like that before . . . kind of like this sand and gravel blasting my shin and calves right now!"

The attendant got the further hint and went from Island work ethic to Chicago work ethic almost exactly as I finished my statement. Within minutes; I am behind the wheel of the Audi and using the stick shift for the first time in approximately twenty years.

I type in Jessica's address on the phone and I notice two routes; one slightly faster than the other. One route heads back towards the airport and along the same road traveled with Gloria in the past two years. I picture all the turns and narrow bridges while using the stick shift.

I'm already rushed because of this storm moving in and figure saving the eight minutes is best; plus I'm on a different path now so why not take a different path!

I follow the directional turn voice guidance; excited to be on my way to see Jessica and to start this winter's excursion.

I find myself re-learning the stick shift fairly easy during the first 30 minutes battling the wind mostly along the road and pulling over briefly to absorb the picturesque view of the ocean from a scenic viewpoint. I'm beginning to believe every point is a scenic viewpoint and feel like this place is actually GOD'S Ultra High Definition.

The storm clouds moving in look fierce though as the palms are flailing in the air above me.

My text to Jessica reads "It's starting to get dark but so far so good. I certainly will not be answering the phone while using the stick shift in these high winds especially along these roads. Still heading in your direction as of now." Just as I start to put the car in gear, her text response alerts the Sat phone. "Stay Safe! They are guessing at this point, I think, but are saying this storm has potential of being one of the largest storms to hit Maui in a very long time!"

The red illuminated clock begins flashing and says 5:55 p.m.
Directly under the clock is the date 1/16/09.
It appears the haze has left Shawn's presence for the first time in a while.

Nervously and abruptly, he finds himself turning on the radio hopeful to get a storm update. Shortly thereafter he hears this "Weather Update Maui County . . . The National Service has extended a Flood ADVISORY for the island of Maui in Maui County until 9 p.m. Radar at 5:24 showed locally heavy rain falling at around 1" per hour along the southeast slope of Haleakala. The area of heavy rain was nearly stationary. Other locations in the Advisory include but are not limited to Kipahulu Gulch, Kaupo and Hamoa. The public is advised to stay away from streams, drainage ditches, and low lying areas prone to flooding. Rainfall and runoff will also cause hazardous driving conditions due to ponding, reduced visibility, and poor braking action. This advisory may need to be extended beyond 9 p.m. if heavy rain persists.

It is as if this advisory and the weather were in perfect sync with one another as the rain starts to fall pretty heavily. I couldn't begin to guess where the other names mentioned during the advisory where located on the island but I knew my travels were taking me through Kaupo at some point along the way.

I am surprised to see the sign to the right of the road at all as the rain continues to pellet off the windshield. To my further surprise, it reads.

"No Rental Cars Beyond This Point!" !

Besides seeing the sign, what I can see further ahead is a continually up and down road with lava sinkholes which appear as bad as any potholes I have ever seen back home.

These sinkholes are different though reminding me of my hometown in many ways at first glance. They are deliberate. They are intentional.

Some are staged prior to their performance; like a Facebook Reality Talk show creating crime while creating crimes themselves type sinkholes.

Plan of attack.

These local land owners who own these cattle and lands here certainly look sketchy to me at this point.

At This Point !

Shoootttzzzz! While reading This Point ! At this point. The Hawaii term "Shooottzz" took on a whole new meaning to me.

This Point ! however; can't be stressed enough!

These points can't be stressed enough it seems as the hissing sound of the land permeates the inside of the Audi.

After rattling it's frame, and embedding itself into the upholstery of the Audi, the hissing sound of This Sign and This Point ! The Thissssss, immediately reminding me of Cali and the rope story.

"Try doing THISSSSSSS!" took on an entire new meaning literally and metaphorically at this point!

"THISSSSS!"

As the HISSSSSIIIING from the Hawaii land and landowners permeates the metal of the frame; I have a visual of my Mustang in customs extensively held and rattled around as if in the hands of King Kong seeing his favorite car enter his land called BoLandO.

I then see a visual of King Kong Shaking my Mustang upside down as if expecting to see ecstasy pills fall from the frame.

I see myself having to extend a car rental for an additional three weeks while shipping my car to Hawaii in the near future.

At This Point ! though I'm stuck on a road following GPS to a destination to see a friend I met at the Grand Opening of "Stingaree".

Between the hissing and the stinging, at this point, my skin became scratchy and itchy. "I haven't felt me own heartbeat (Irish version).

It's hardly real; the light in my eyes . . ." as the thunder crashes down directly atop This Point ! The beastly head of Thisssss hisssing snake is zapped in mid air moments before King Kong was about to stand up.

The lava was getting a certain glow to it and the smell of burnt rubber was in the air. Mind you this was after rolling backwards down one of the hills as if the rented Audi was a skateboard at a skatepark.

Somewhere in this scenario the car had died out because I forgot to switch gears as I was just about to get to the top of the hill.

I BEGIN ROLLING BACKWARDS AS THE CAR DIES OUT! It rolls down the hill I was just about to edge over and then back up the hill I had already gone down.

Feeling like a pinball losing its momentum; I begin to sway back and forth between the two hills. The massive lightning strike atop the Serpent's head distracted me while driving shortly after seeing my Mustang in the hand of King Kong shaking it I would imagine.

I have just taken a very deep breath after slamming on the breaks once I felt safe to stop the pinball momentum the Audi had created.

I begin to roll down the window and the stench of burnt rubber seems to embed itself into the metal of the Audi's frame.

The heated lava begins to glow even more. As the head of the hisssing snake crashes down to This Point ! on the land directly in front of me, reminding me of Halloween Night when the Escalade and Durango collided.

It was at this smoked filled rubber embed moment on Maui when "Shoootzzz", the Hawaii term, became to have more meaning to me than ever before! As the s becomes a z and the z becomes an s. "SHoootzzz!"

The cattle and land here are important and some of these landowners violate rights of others. Meaning; some go far beyond their legal rights of cattle and land ownership. Add to the fact that they have been given the legal use of guns on these properties.

These cattle are sometimes more than just cattle too; local woman, their flock if you will, act as "their land informants"

Anyways, I find my mind wondering what to do. I call Jessica and explain to her the roads I'm on and she feels like I have gotten off track because I should not be seeing these signs! She again stresses "to be careful!" she says "there are reports of trees down so the roads may be blocked at some point if the tree limb is too big to move!"

"Big Tree limbs are Hard to Move in Storms especially!" Jessica expresses with a deep care and concern in her voice.

While saying goodbye and disconnecting from the Sat call Shawn begins to pray: "God, it feels like I have been stuck at This Point ! for awhile here and yet this point has not been clearly established yet. So, I am going to do my best to continue on. I have regained my breath completely and am beginning to feel the heartbeat in my chest again.

So, thank you! I appreciate you and the angels watching over me during these travels!" The rain completely stops as the glow and steam from the lava lessons considerably.

King Kong is laying down comfortably now as if he is on a bed of heated stone as Zissafiss' whistle blowing softens after already flexing and bending the air molecules creating a very unique flexing of the atmosphere; similar to the sound of a fighter jet at take off. The point in the air it seems to blast thru and yet take off from is the point not yet clearly to be made in this book; referenced above at This Point !

Stingaree and Stingray are the interpretations of Zissafiss' two clicks written in the galaxy air in front of me. The two clicks repeat, creating two more clicks and two more clicks until the Two Voices of Nuwa and Noah are faintly heard in the distance talking over each other and one another too each other in considerable fashion but both from another to another.

Nuwa says, "Remember, God has not given you the spirit of fear, you're not alone!"

Noah says, "Remember, Jessica is watching one of the Hawaiian elders' homes!" Both of them end their messages by saying the same thing in unison "If you need to explain yourself to one of the property owners- they can always call Jessica as a reference! 11:11 Make a Wish!"

This clearly reminded me of a call I received at my office by one of the landowners which hasn't even existed yet; but at this point I am ready to absorb anything.

I think Durango Vs. Escalade sounds like a great Fury Tyson; like a Teddy Bear if you will. I mean- come on; the blows of the baseball bat, the Mustang Missile, the detaching of the back break on my custom Bourget Kruzer, the golf balls pinging of my house, the dead pigeon left on the sidewalk- all of those things leading to the informant infiltrated girlfriend who is involved in a Facebook Reality TV show named "iD and gaD"?

Ticky-Tacky Take 1) The landowner says on the other line as I answer, "Shawn, there's an Egyptian belly dancer involved in what appears to be a very disturbing Human

Trafficking Case. When asked if she knew of a reference locally whom she trusted; her response was "your name and your number." The landowner continues; " Are you willing to pick her up upon her request even though we are a few hours North of you?"

I immediately said, "yes" and made plans for a decent car ride then and now amidst these two different but similar land owner scenarios.

The rain begins to fall abruptly again but the up and down lava sinkhole infested roads are behind me now (at least at this point along the road it seems).

Eventually the rain subsides as I find myself 11 minutes away from Jessica's property.

I power the driver window down and the ocean waves to the left of me are intoxicatingly tranquil! It appears there is the porch light flashing yet all other homes look dark. Jessica has no idea how I am coming up from the opposite direction while we are talking on the phone but that's her outside with the flashlight while saying, "the ocean should be on your right!"

Jessica is happy I made it and has absolutely no idea how. She heard on television that many trees were down blocking the road prior to the power going out hours ago.

The conversation and the bottle of wine is refreshing as I make my way towards the back bedroom. Upon walking in I see two full size mattresses in a L-shape to the left of the patio door leading to an outdoor deck. To the right of it I see a night stand and clothes rack.

Jessica begins to tell me more about the property and the elder who owns the home by saying a lot to me in the next few minutes. Surprisingly I'm following her story completely because it is simply fascinating.

Come closer. Feel free to listen in to what she says: "many of the elders like himself are gathering together for the first time in many years with multiple other elders of other Hawaiian families. Some of which continue to live on the land and others like himself who have not visited the land in quite some time.

The Elders and many offspring of their families are fed up with many things happening around them.

1) Many Hawaiians have to work two jobs to survive the rising costs and some have to work three.

2) Hawaii used to be self sustaining with few imports yet those statistics have completely flip flopped.

3) More of their land is being bought up and more resorts are being built.

a) Oprah bought more than 200 acres of coastal land on Hana between 2002 and 2005. In my opinion it is some of the most beautiful property on Hawaii.

b) Larry Ellison, the co-founder of Oracle bought 98% of the entire island of Lanai in 2012 for 300 million with future plans of it becoming 100% self sustaining on a futuristic scale.

4) Hawaiians especially do not like white American males especially. After all it was a white American male, Captain Cook, who put a gun to the queen's head demanding the land become U.S territory. Interestingly enough the queen added a preclusion to the

proposal prior to the signing of it which basically said " purchasers of the land are strictly care keepers of the land because all land is owned by the Hawaiian people!"

Jessica laughs a little bit before saying ... "As a result Shawn; over the course of your stay, you will often hear locals referring to you as 'Haole'. It means man without spirit or man without breath."

"Shawn, are you catching all this?" Jessica asks? Shawn replies, " The flight and the drive over hit me harder than Tyson or Tyson when he is Fury but I think I actually do."

Jessica says, "I know you're tired but explain it back to me so I know you were listening ...this is important!"

Shawn says, "in a nutshell; the Elders have and are constructively fighting for their sovereignty from the United States meeting more and more often. You work for one of those elders by managing his home and property. Hawaiians believe white American's have no breath or spirit primarily because of Captain Cook so they will be calling me names."

The last thing I hear Jessica say after "very good listening Chicago Shawn" are the words "wraparound deck" as I get lost in the sound of the ocean waves. They are peacefully breaking across the street echoing off the mountains out the open patio door next to Jessica's bed.

I wake up around 9:00 a.m Chicago time which if I'm doing the time change thingy correctly; it is 5:00 a.m. Hawaii time. Jessica looks sound to sleep but I'm excited to see the sunrise and property in the morning light.

I grab my sandals which are by the patio door. Hawaiian culture believe in leaving shoes by the doors. It helps protect against bringing evil entities into the home.

In fact I learned most Hawaiians will actually let their sandals wait in line for them as they sit. The sandals represent their bodies standing. Occasionally the sandals need to get moved to more of the front of the original start line but it is a fairly decent modification to actually waiting in line while standing.

I am tippy toeing through the kitchen which appears to be more of a log cabin resort style kitchen as opposed to a home.

I'm facing the ocean and stepping on the wrap around deck for the first time in the day and find myself posting a video on Facebook entitled " 22 Seconds in Heaven!"

A beautiful Lava Mountain sits abruptly in the ocean which can be seen from an angle of approx 145-160 degrees. There is a fairly narrow freshly paved road between the front lawn and the ocean's sand.

I stop recording the video at 22 seconds and walk to the end of the deck to my right. Looking towards the backyard I see the landscape has bushes with beautiful flowers planted in a heart shape better defining the shorter grass portion of the vast property. It stretches as far back as the massive mountain behind it starts; most certainly God's Ultra HD!

Jessica walks towards me with two coffees in hand and within minutes begins apologizing about blasting me with all the Hawaiian details at the end of a long night. She is assuring me not to worry about the Hawaiian hatred for white guys by saying "once I introduce you to them while sharing my dog's story and you and your cousin Vince's involvement; they will most definitely take you in as one of their own!" I laugh telling her, "that is the last thing on my mind while seeing you for the first time in the daylight along with this beautiful home you are managing. I believe the proper Hawaii term I should be saying to you is 'Aloha'! "

I learn the next Elderly Hawaii weekend shindig is scheduled for tomorrow as a large white truck briefly stops on the road in front of the home.

Jessica runs into the kitchen and is out front quickly with a pretty thick envelope she's handing the driver.

She begins telling me he is going to attempt to drive back towards the airport since the nearest Costco is there and is hopeful the roads are cleared of any major debris before he gets there. It's his weekly trip into town for major supplies and with the expected gathering tomorrow; the town is in desperate need of supplies.

She still is baffled by seeing me come from the other direction last night but is glad the car and myself made it without harm.

Most of the day she is busy planning for the event while I'm catching up on sleep on a towel on the beach in front of the home; while sipping on Kona Brewery Beers. Some of the stares I have been getting by a couple people on the back of flatbed trucks passing by have me a bit off kilter while they happen. I admit to being a bit nervous about meeting many of the locals as a result of Jessica's stories and these stares. For the most part, I go on throughout the day without giving it much thought; primarily because of the peaceful scenery and the jet lag which creeps in with the hot afternoon sun.

I am fast asleep well before Jessica enters the room at night but the next morning wake peacefully slightly early by island standards.

The ocean waves soothe my ears and arise with energy to help out if at all needed for today's events.

I plan on getting my foot in the door quickly with some of the local's while helping Jessica once she awakens.

For the most part everyone seems to be awkwardly comfortable with the new guy helping out after learning I will be staying for awhile on the Hana side but I'm still waiting for Jessica to share the story.

We have most everything set up fairly early in the afternoon and honestly it has been a great start to the vacation. Much later and after meeting several people the elder of the property arrives there along with most everyone else who will be attending.

Jessica begins to introduce me further sharing the story of how we met along with the beginning of her dog situation prior to being able to move here.

Most everyone is laughing at this point while I'm standing next to her feeling slightly embarrassed but the vibe from the majority of everyone there seems more positive than before she started to share the story.

After mentioning my last name, things got as different for Jessica as they did for an escort I knew named Ashley, while she was being arrested by the local police department.

They both begin getting bombarding questions with respect to my last name.

There are a lot of people asking more details to both of them rather than directing those questions to me.

The elder of the home I am staying at turns to me after quieting the group and says, "Your last name is Bosi and you're from the Chicago area?"

Nervously Shawn responds, "yes that's correct! Why do you ask?" He politely introduces himself and afterwards asks, " do you have any relation to Frank Bosi from the Chicago land area? "

Even more nervous; I find myself fumbling for words for a bit and laughing a little bit before saying, "yes- Frank is one of my favorite uncles actually. He used to race cars!"

Immediately he begins raising his hands in excitement and says a couple of words to other elders under his breath. Those older elders lean over to some younger elders and begin whispering to them and Jessica is barely making eyes contact with me at the moment.

I start to reminisce about the times in the past when people have asked me of my relations with Vince, Hank, Art, etc. and it's a love em or leave em last name in my opinion. I have found as many fans of the Bosi's as I have found haters on the other side of those questions.

This question and ensuing response has me on edge more than most though as two of the younger and much bigger Hawaiians walk towards one of the tall wood cabinets and are about to open them. Without knowing the meaning; Jessica smiles at me. I believe she's trying to stay positive but it certainly sends mixed signals in my direction.

My heart stops a bit as the haze enters my body for the first time from behind me unknowingly at first. I feel the vibrant energy squeeze through my back filling my body as the cabinet door opens.

As the two men turn around they have bottles of some very good alcohol in both of their hands: a Blue Label Johnnie Walker, Grey Goose, Hibiki, and a Don Julio 1942!

Go to find out; several of the elders present at this party had met with and partied with Frank on multiple occasions when he would accompany Al Capone to Hana.

The drinks were getting poured and the celebration was underway! I was in with the locals. Somewhere in between the 10'th and 15'th shot the elder that matter leaned over saying " you're welcome to stay in any of the open rooms on the property for as long as you want. Besides having to rotate rooms occasionally depending upon other paid guests coming in and out- that will be the only hassles you have on this island!"

The elder begins laughing while saying" Cheers to our Hawaiian families reuniting with the Bosi's again!" Laughing hysterically, he yells louder than any other time of the night saying "This Bosi drove a rental car through private cattle country during one of the most severe storms this island has seen!"

At this moment Jessica and I actually understood why I had come from the opposite direction she had expected and why the ocean was on my left while approaching the property. I knew nothing about cattle country until this moment although referenced before.

Most of the locals look at me in amazement saying, "you drove thru cattle country in a rental car during that storm two nights ago? Props for not only taking that route but actually making it through!"

Upon hearing them voice this to me in laughter, I begin to see the correlation of the event and me actually writing a further addition to my book!

The Hawaiian herb is as plentiful as the top shelf alcohol for the remainder of the celebration.

I must have been about as high as a hot air balloon in the clearing net because the next thing I know I'm at the Four Seasons Resort on the Kona side of The Big Island. Unfortunately it is not Christmas, I'm not swimming in the lagoons while waiting to see

Cameron Diaz or Jim Carry, so deductive reasoning tells me this is definitely not the time I was thrown off of the property and banned from staying at the resort in any fashion for one year.

Ticky Tack Take 2) I'm waiting out front in my Mustang after having been called by one of my closest island friends, named Tiffany, she was hysterically begging for me to come and get her.

She has been spending a lot of time with an Emmy Award winning writer who has a plush ocean view home and guest house there. Earlier today Tiffany was insisting on asking him if I can come there and join her in the guest house for one or several overnight stays.

Even though she continues to explain how nice and understanding he is of our friendship she has developed with me over the last month, I am a bit skeptical.

I never intended on being on Hawaii myself with the Mustang. I shipped it over last year during a 4 1/2 month stay entitled "No Bills No Pills."

This time was referenced earlier in the story about the extended stay my car had in costumes while King Kong shook it upside down trying to get ecstasy pills to drop from the frame.

At the same time my workman's compensation check of $1,243.92 weekly was cut off and my newly hired attorney said "in the past it has taken over a year to get previous client's benefits turned back on!"

Mind you I had over $10,0000 a month in bills for myself and my business with no money coming in. Three months ago the mortgage modification fell thru last minute because the weekly compensation check I was receiving "could not be deemed income" per their standards. They knew these checks were workman's compensation checks at the beginning of the process but they drag me thru a yearlong modification process asking for documentation as to where certain large deposits came from etc.

Hours and hours of time spent and wham the implosion begins as the modification is declined which only exacerbated the foreclosure filing into Sheriff's Sale of the home/shop/office I designed and built for myself and business.

Mind you; I have been diagnosed with Avascular Necrosis in both hips, a labral tear of the tendon stretching across the hip, and at least one or two lower back herniated discs from the work injury.

The bank and insurance companies' decisions impacted me financially and started to impair my health even more so until I broke free from the anxiety, worry and stress. I started to live by the principles I express while writing the earlier stages of this book.

Instead of staying stuck in all the surrounding negativity which was being created at times intentionally by a local cabal; I become more thankful! More thankful of the teachers, business owners, editors, doctors, lawyers, attorneys, private investigators, eventually judges and even President Trump; all of which help enlighten my path.

That's right; Trump has gone from hosting Dennis Rodman on "Celebrity Apprentice" to President in this timeframe.

"Shootzzz" as the Hawaii locals would say!

Even the dependency I developed to pain medications while receiving treatment for my injury was added to the gratitude list.

I sold all my stock for mostly losses at the time and started planning the 3 1/2 month trip which later became 4 1/2 months. I stopped taking all the pills they were readily handing me and I stopped paying all my bills.

Within the first week of being on the island; Tiffany and I met. Let's just say for the sake of the story she was hitchhiking when I picked her up.

One month later; Tiffany tells me Mr. Emmy Award winner is happy for her and us but my brain simply has a hard time wrapping my head around those concepts together after everything I have experienced.

Based upon the fear in her voice begging me to come and get her; I am imagining it did not go well at all.

I race there faster than any other time traveling in the past only to hear both of the front desk attendants say at different times, "there are no registered guests visiting the person's last name you provided me with sir- so there's nothing we can do!"

It doesn't take me long to respond back with, "I know Tiffany is in there whether her name is on the guest list or not and I'm not leaving until she is with me. Do what you need to accommodate her safe return or I will be contacting The Hawaii Police shortly!"

Obviously; they are like King Kong anywhere on Hawaii and not welcomed often at a multimillion dollar home of an Emmy Award Winning author.

I wait approx one hour continually trying to call Tiffany and continually talking with different people stirring up a bit of commotion using this person's last name.

Tiffany appears walking with a bit of a limp. Her hair is a mess. Her eye makeup entirely smeared and she is practically hyperventilating while she is hugging me crying like a found lost puppy.

This image becomes a mirrored reflection of one of the meetings I will have with the Egyptian belly dancer at my property somewhere in the future before the landowner calls me and asks if I will pick her up.

It's almost an identical mirrored reflection as she approaches me limping then hugging me while crying with heavy smeared eye makeup down her cheek. She asks me if she can clean up a bit before telling me what happened.

In the meantime; it looks like whoever dropped her off has fallen off the edge of my driveway and cannot get enough traction in the snow/ice to spin forward. I hurry to put on my coat and surprise the shit out of the driver as I ask" hey man- what's is going on? . . . she limped past me crying and at the same time I saw you fall off the driveway!" The driver doesn't go into a detailed explanation besides saying "she is having a bad night and just received a terrible phone call before going into your house."

I ask him if he wants me to push him out slowly with my truck and he nods his head in agreement.

By the time I go inside Miss Egyptian has cleaned up fast but is in a towel. Shortly thereafter she begins to show me the road rash from being thrown out of the car at over 30 mph. I ask her if the guy in the car was her boyfriend and she said "no, it's his brother and tonight he found out some things he did not like about me so he threw me out of the car!"

I told her she was welcome to stay with me for as long as she needed to get her life in order. Fast forward one month and her and I are surprisingly visited by two car loads of people. Her and I were shooting pool in my game room at the time they showed up in my backyard and front yard.

At this point! the snakes were certainly hissing but they had already slid open the patio door and we were severely outnumbered. I was talking to them all as calmly as possible and making sure they were going to remain civil while in my home. I begin offering them beers and chicken recently made and in the stove.

I could tell things were off by her actions. Plus, the majority of my collectibles were skewed on the walls suggesting they were all checked to determine how they attached to the wall while I was not in my room.

She makes an excuse to go and poor a bath and one of the guys is gone longer than expected so I decide to make sure she is ok. I turn the corner of my master bedroom and see him standing on top of her feet on the tiles of my heated bathroom floor. He easily doubles her in weight and is approx a foot and a half taller than her. I immediately say, "come on bud...you told me this was going to be a civil meeting so standing on her feet definitely crosses the line."

He leaves her to soak in the Jacuzzi she is pouring and exits with me as we both walk back to the pool room.

Fifteen minutes later a loud spraying from the jets is heard in between the music we are listening to. I'm concerned because it sounds like the jets are on but the water is not high enough and it could be spraying all over the heated tiles. He begins ahead of me towards the sound in the bathroom and as I turn the bathroom corner he is standing there dumbfounded with water spraying everywhere.

The window by the tub is open and the screen is removed. Miss Egyptian is gone in the night and not heard from or seen ever, until the random call, from the landowner asking if I would be willing to pick her up.

Tiffany however does not want to talk about the experience at all. She boldly says, "I will not be seeing that asshole ever again!"

The entire car ride home she is drifting off somewhere else crying on and off without saying a word. Within a month later; my entire car is drifting off the road faster than a speeding bullet. It is traveling too fast for the curve while being chased by a low rider and smaller car filled with people looking to do me harm.

Earlier in the chase I had listened to the earlier voice in this story encouraging me "To Slow Down". I knew the low rider was chasing me and I knew it had something to do with Tiffany so I decided to pull over to the right of the road and start to get out to see what this guy wants.

Upon pulling over; I notice not only is there the low rider but it appears to be a mini coop behind it which has also just pulled over. I see at least two doors open on both vehicles so I already know the outnumbered feeling while experiencing it again.

That's why I decide to take off but without knowing I was literally about to take off.

I make it through several aggressive turns with the tires squealing while adding a decent distance between myself and the aggressors but don't realize the hairpin turn to the left until my real (eyes) now know it was too late.

The Mustang acting more like a surfboard at this time swooshed up and to the left. I find myself screaming out loud, " oh my God please help me !" at the same time I close my eyes.

There's a forceful crash back into the atmosphere after the car has twisted in mid air at least once. There's smoke and fog everywhere as I first open my eyes and glance thru the shattered but intact windshield. The airbag has not deployed. The rear glass is completely gone. The driver door will not open; so after taking off my seatbelt; I find myself kicking the door to get it open. Just as I'm getting out of the vehicle I hear two people run up saying " Oh my God , You came from out of the sky like a missile! Where did you come from? "

I wasn't quick enough to say "another galaxy" nor have I experienced the time travel galaxy phenomenon at that point in my life so all I could say was, "Down there; I came from down there! Do you see where those headlights are turning around? I came from down there and those are the guys who were chasing me!"

While being loaded into an ambulance I hear the same woman saying, "He shot out of the sky like a missile!"

The landowner responds, "ahhhhh the Mustang Missile was referenced earlier on a Reality TV show I was watching last night... I forget the name though: 'Ig and Dug' or something like that. They must be kind of like the Simpsons predicting events before they occur.

CHAPTER XVI

THE MISSILE ALERT

Wikipedia Reference:
Incident: The Missile Alert.
January 13'th 2018

The alert was sent at 8:07 a.m. Hawaii–Aleutian Standard Time. [27] People in Hawaii reported seeing the alert on their smart phones. Many screenshots of the push alert were shared on social media platforms, such as Twitter. [28][29] The alert read, in all capital letters:[30] BALLISTIC MISSILE THREAT INBOUND TO HAWAII. SEEK IMMEDIATE SHELTER. THIS IS NOT A DRILL. Local television broadcasts, including a college basketball game between Florida and Ole Miss being shown on CBS affiliate KGMB and a Premier League match between Tottenham Hotspur and Everton on NBC affiliate KHNL were also interrupted by a similar alert message, broadcast as a Civil Danger Warning. [31][32][33] The alert message on television broadcasts took the form of both an audio message and a scrolling banner. It stated in part:[34] The U.S. Pacific Command has detected a missile threat to Hawaii. A missile may impact on land or sea within minutes. THIS IS NOT A DRILL. If you are indoors, stay indoors. If you are outdoors, seek immediate shelter in a building. Remain indoors well away from windows. If you are driving, pull safely to the side of the road and seek shelter in a building or lay on the floor. We will announce when the threat has ended. THIS IS NOT A DRILL. Take immediate action measures. An alert message also interrupted radio broadcasts in the state.[35][36] In Lihue, a resident reported hearing a message on the radio advising of "an incoming missile warning for the islands of Kauai and Hawaii".[37

By this time, I figured to have experienced all I could, but this imminent threat comes blasting thru my Sat phone after a very late night out on the Kona side of the Big Island.

I'm having much difficulty falling back asleep after reading it. I hear children screaming outside as some parents begin lifting the sewer drains and telling their children to get down there.

I walk outside to see my roommate playing the guitar softly while his buddy prepares a couple lines on the table in front of him. I say "Shoootz braddahs - if This Is It then we mind as well go down in style!"

I open the freezer and grab the chilled bottle of Crown Apple while immediately opening the refrigerator for three Modelo bottles to act as chasers since it is a bit early (per Hawaii standards especially).

We drink a little and smoke a little more in between conversing. My roommate gets a call from one of his Maui friends rhapsodizing, "We all just saw a missile get shot down into the ocean here so hopefully this means we will all remain safe... if not; I love you braddah- Shoootz!"

It's a quick call with a lot of commotion going on in the backdrop but I'm guessing it was approximately 30 minutes after the original missile alert warning was sent.

Officially 8:45 (Thirty-eight minutes and 13 seconds later) everyone is told it is a false alarm. For days, weeks and months after the missile alert peeps were told it was an on off switch toggled mistakenly in the wrong direction. Some of the most valuable real estate in America and yet the missile alert system is an on off switch?

Honestly; let's get real with the things we are seeing across the world because it seems a lot like . . . a gender dysphoria.

A lot of people like seeing Dennis Rodman going from being on "Celebrity Apprentice" with host of the show Donald Trump to meeting with supreme leader Kim Jong Un in North Korea with Donald Trump as President of the U.S.

Less than six months after "The Missile Alert"; Dennis Rodman is with President Donald Trump meeting with Kim Jong Un in North Korea.

Hyyymmmm; sounds like a Facebook Reality TV show but this isn't amateur hour.

Deductive reasoning along with my own experiences coupled with the private jet reports of Donald Trump's flight the day of the missile threat leads me to believe Trump's plane was shot at by a missile. Thus, The Missile Alert! Let's assume for a second China tried to assassinate a sitting president who continued to say they are massive manipulators of currency along with a number of other things.

Let's assume China wanted to make it appear to come from North Korea in hopes Trump will swiftly retaliate.

China deliberately has kept the price of Bitcoin down for years because they are currency manipulators as referenced by Trump on a multitude of occasions throughout his campaign.

Notice the mass advertising campaign designed by our Reality TV guru President with respect to Bitcoin in his first year as president.

Bitcoin is advertised on a very large majority of all of our television programs, Facebook, and Twitter while the price of it races in one year from under $950.00 to $20,000.00 by the end of the same year in 2017.

Now China tries to take out Trump with a missile but no one is told about it. Instead; it's kept on the down low unlike the advertising of Bitcoin.

Thirteen days into the New Year of 2018 and Trump's plane is shot at by a missile.

Then the SEC kindly shuts down USI-Tech and all Americans who purchased Bitcoin thru USI-Tech are left with nothing to show for it. The price of Bitcoin plummets down 65% from January 6'th to February 6'th 2018. The SEC Blocks Chinese Takeover of The Chicago Stock Exchange Feb. 15'th, 2018.

China's Long March Through Institutions which started 100 years ago ironically is called "Long March Through Institutions". The steps are slow and deliberate. 1/1, 2/2, 3/3, and 4/4. Chinese and American!

Speaking of deliberate steps; did the activity at Puna Geothermal Venture (PGV) influence the Kilauea volcano's East Rift Zone eruption that lasted from May 3 to September 4'th, 2018 on The Big Island?

At the time; Trump is a real estate mogul president being pressured by Hawaiian elders for their land to be separate from the U.S. "Their land can't become anymore separate from the U.S. than it already is because it's very expensive cattle land where only the imagination and reality can merge to better understand Everything Under Ground and Under Guidance is Under the Surveillance Of KING KONG!"; I recall having a heated argument with Jessica.

Some of the elders saying, "I respect the queen's preclusion with respect to the ownership of land remaining property of the Hawaiian's, but Hawaii is a key strategic position for the U.S. military and I do not see the U.S Government ever letting the state go!"

I wish the above reference was actually said by some of the elders but it was actually me saying it to them! I put on a tremendous performance while carrying a mini recording device into their merger of the Facebook Reality TV show as it was transitioning into a very sophisticated Hell's Kitchen Parody Porno called " Creating Crime to Create Crime; While Creating Crime ".

To me there are way too many references to Crime in the name of their production but you know these producers in this chain strongly feel crime sells. Allow a bunch of people to get hyped on MMA fighting so the Agenda of The Domestic Violence programs can really reap the reward years later. "More fights in general lead to more arrests. Crime Sells because Crime Cells are created and because of the crime cells created; the crime cells will be more full. "

Now that's a mouthful but this particular elder's voice of opinion is not done yet as he begins hissing in between his statements. I mean actually hisssing! "Hisssssssssss, Hisssssssss, Hisssssss . . . What was seen and experienced was unlike anything before as the much hotter lava poured itself hissing into the ocean. There was much more fluid and was much more fast moving with 24 fissures erupting in an area of about a mile of PGV.

What are the chances that 24 fissures erupt within a mile of PGV by coincidence?

Nuwa walks towards me and divides himself in half while taking military style steps towards me and Nowa. The steps are slow and deliberate. 1/1, 2/2, 3/3, and 4/4.

Chinese and American!

Chase bank shorts silver because China has 1 of the Top 3 silver reserves and is 1 of the world's largest 3 silver producers; if I recall properly

The Chinese strategy includes infiltrations through the NBA, TIK TOK and Institutes on U.S soil run by The Chinese Communist Party. I believe Confucius Institutes sprouted up to more than 500 college campuses by January 16, 2018. I'd have to check to see how many allowed Bitcoin to fund their education but Bitcoin funds other college educations here in the U.S. (Not any Bitcoin bought thru USI-Tech while many Americans were using it as a source to buy it though...that's no bueno and is worth nothing. It just disappeared! Swooosh; like a tablecloth into a magician's hand. You see it really didn't disappear at all even though USI-Tech Bitcoin is not even a bit of a coin at all!

Our Freedoms "cannot" be like that tablecloth disappearing but still there. They are not Freedumbs!

American ends in "I Can".

The Chinese strategy includes a collaboration with useful idiots and the 50 Million to Hunter and The Bidens is just a gift.

On top of all that, China is buying up U.S farmland and police stations.

Landowners of U.S. farmland and police stations? Maybe The Bidens may just suggest who some of those useful idiots are and where this Confucius Cattle Cop mentality stems from.

Maybe " Bi Den " was the name of the Facebook Reality TV show where the "If You Will $10,000.00 Bribe" may have escalated this whole mess eight days after I was born as a Courtesy Done by Dunn C. Curtis. Joe was sworn in to the Senate at the hospital two weeks later.

When everything is underground you gotta dig deeper with a good light and a sat phone. I recommend the flexible snake light and the Iridium Extreme in Sporting Camo sat phone. I have a feeling a may have to own one for the first time once this book is published.

When everything hidden becomes known; please refer to Luke and earlier poem. On top of all that China is buying up U.S farmland and police stations. Land owners of U.S. farmland and police stations . . .

"Landowners of cattle property and police stations." The two voices were deliberate as they speak to me;

"Landowners of cattle property and police stations.

The two voices are deliberate because they speak to me! The Crystal Rope of Two Choices heard from Two Voices lead me too 2 Things (Deuces Wild); neither of which were learned by Confucius as I attended The University of Florida.

Emmitt Smith was already playing for The Cowboy's but had promised his grandmother he'd finish his degree so he was there too.

Wait, "What is Emmitt Smith's retired jersey number?" Come On . . . #22 ! Deuces Wild with 3 exclamation points ! ! !

I had to add at least one for myself because of the 2 things which came to me after my deep breath. These two people, these two voices uniquely connect my business world and personal world together.

My relationship and relationships to these two things and within these two things all coincide together creating a harmonious conclusion. It leaves banks to get leveraged further out of their money or it provides options for them to do business with people who are trying to employ others with their hard-earned dollars and efforts. It's an offer of restitute for the readers and other people struggling like me. A savings grace needed for people experiencing issues like myself. Believe me; I certainly know these issues and or experiences will not be verbatim to mine but for many the underlying issues are definitely the same.

I started by doing these Two Things as my best response to the many of the games played and "Dreamality" formed as the object placed in the slingshot against the world. It became my only answer.

Two Things

Find a quiet place and Lose yourself in prayer

I promise if you do these two things He will be there!

Reflect in nature and with pets

Learn to live with no regrets

Reach out to others and laugh more

Cuz, you have no idea what he has in store

Never lose hope and Live in the Light

Take less than what you give, and you'll have true sight

Take care of yourself and remember to breathe

Don't be afraid. . . You can fall to your knees

Listen to music, Listen to him

Ask for forgiveness of your sins and listen to him. (or them as in my case)!

CHAPTER XVII

DA LION'S DEN

Shootzzzz; as the s becomes a z and the z becomes a s as I hear the words "DA Lion's Den" said together by Zissafiss and a 'SJJ' Mermaid named Babydoll Madison Star.

I don't necessarily remember how exactly this moment has been created but it was, and it did. It did and it was. I don't know if it was what it was or it was what I was on but I haven't drank any Climax moonshine yet and yet I am feeling the Climax is fast approaching.

No, I'm not referencing that type of climax either although seeing her definitely heightened my surrounding awareness.

Zissafiss has brought me to this place. He has uniquely and categorically introduced us both by abruptly shifting the playing field while leaving some details quite symmetrical. More importantly disappearing without explaining much of anything to me, except for our names, has me baffled.

Symmetry in Nature as usual for him I guess; but for me it is so much more as I can barely keep my breath underwater without the need to keep my breath underwater as she continues to say, "Green Eyes; I sure hope you are as ready to enter Da Den together as Zissafiss has explained to me! Again, I'm Babydoll Madison Star and this is Da Lion's Den. I'm excited to meet you finally!"

" Hi Babydoll! May I call you Babydoll or does Madison Star need to follow it while addressing you?" Shawn asks.

Babydoll Madison Star replies, " that's most definitely fine! Tell me something about yourself please."

Mind you, Shawn has been able to breathe entirely fine under water with Zissafiss in the past so I certainly think Babydoll has caught his breath while he attempts to speak. I think he got lost in her eyes as they are the same color of the ocean behind her and is lost with her southern yet hip Chicago tone in her voice.

"I'm a Southsider of Chicago so Da Sox, Da Bulls and Da Raiderz are my teams! I am a business owner/ author/ entrepreneur/penny stock trader/ aspiring artist and never been married. I own an American Staffordshire Terrier who looks like a stuffed animal from Disney but has the nickname "Beastie" for very good reason. I have not before met a mermaid- so excuse me if you had me at whatever word or words you said first that I may not have heard. You're strikingly beautiful and have a nice tail... I'm sorry if saying it is still offensive here.

" The 'SJJ' mermaid begins to laugh while saying " do you like my curves and edges?"

Before Shawn had time to respond or better yet said; before he heard another one of her words he heard the word "Zissafiss".

Shawn says, 'did you say Zissafiss?'

Babydoll responds, "yes I was about to say; Zissafiss knew years ago. You see; I have been praying for a while now to meet a man who was in the top one percent. I had further hopes he would have a great bond with his dog and we would form a Trinity inclusive of Zissafiss at all times."

I'm lost for words while we transcend into one another's deepest layers within our eyes as I begin to realize where I might be - so I stutter while asking, " Is Da Da Da Lion's Den part of the underwater city of Atlantis?"

The 'SJJ' mermaid responds with laughter saying, "No silly, in many ways it's like the Private Cove on Hawaii you were blessed to have experienced. No Mermaid has ever told of these places of existence to another species and unless first introduced by Zissafiss- there is no way of getting here. It's our mermaid secret kept between mermaids! Plus, this one as are all- is specifically designed for you. "

Shawn asks, " why is it called 'Da Lion's Den' ?"

Babydoll responds , "Because your dog, hopefully our dog- will guard it going forward in the future! 'SJJ' mermaids are categorized as similar to Lionesses in many fashions (especially when above ground).

More importantly it is a constant Hawaii/ Chicago style reminder of the bible story when David got tossed into The Lion's Den and came out unharmed!"

My mind had a very difficult time comprehending everything she was saying but thanks to the mini recorder I know I can play it back in the future. Last I recall her saying after hearing the words 'Crystal Ropes' was "Big Tree Limbs are easily moved here even during a storm, the water is always warm and the sun is always shining."

Besides being a super attractive mermaid, I have no idea how Babydoll Madison Star has been able to allow me to forget all which has been happening to me prior to Zissafiss having brought me here. I was trying not to think of everything which I had experienced but nothing on earth was helping me besides prayer and writing. Occasionally I would be lost in work and responsibilities but even then and especially then and now most of everything had merged because of the cabal leader of this entire orchestrated scheme. A scheme of which has been ongoing in my life for over two years (at least this one that is).

The catfish scheme on Facebook from the model on contract not allowed to share video or have video calls was run by a woman in this cabal because her dad was pretty high up in the organization before deciding to race cars. I think my last name meant more to him at the time because of my uncle Frank but that's another unknown.

I am laughing now because going from a catfish to a mermaid is a huge leap even while in a "Dreamality underwater galaxy" but at This Point ! ; I would need to go back to gain access to that part of my brain and while looking into her deep blue eyes this is . .

HOW I FEEL

I am sometimes overwhelmed with her eyes of blue shining
As a result ; all I can do is smile and thank the Lord above
Reflections of myself in her I see , not looking yet finding
Understanding entirely her definition of the word love .

Yet mine, though different appears to be one in the same
For my love is sought with the pursuit of wisdom
Realizing the more I give - directly relates to what I gain
True knowledge is where the bridge of faith begins from .

Experiencing the day as if there may be no tomorrow ,
Using what I have learned in the past as a touch tone for growth .
Not regretting those mistakes which may have caused me sorrow
For without the darkness of pain , one cannot experience the light in hope .
In an effort to thank - for the opportunity that has been granted
These words from my heart are written for this 'SJJ' Mermaid .
Communicating with her on this level ; I am truly enchanted
True feelings expressed with nothing concealed.

Oh, I forgot to mention that thoughts become written words here as well so the teal letters are floating in the waves now in front of me and her. They highlight more the longer they catch the wave, but they can also wait patiently and wait to " Catch Da Next Wave Up!" very similar to penny stocks. Most contestants in "The Third Annual Race to Da Penny" have the ability to race 30 X higher on average and when those letters and numbers are that high on the wave, they are such a solid green. Eventually they become a very vibrant orange as they become silver on land in our near future.

$ilver is one of the most undervalued asset right now. Please make sure your bank vaults are properly covered with insurance because the brighter the greenish orangish color it becomes as it gets brighter and higher in the wave it becomes $ilver! As bright as the top of the Big Wave as the sun pierces it.

The puppets silver strings appear to be absorbed by a waterspout as if the waterspout were baby and younger spinner dolphins enjoying the early morning, performing theatrical spins and twists; while catching some surprised flying bugs: As if Crystal Ropes appear between their eyes !

Even while looking underwater the sunlight pierces and heats the top of the wave and the hissing of the land even the hissing of the lava as it contacts the ocean; all the hissing is silenced at the top of the next major $ilver wave. Please go back to the last time you see future. $ilver together: everything after that is the energy high and the feeling her and I both get as Babydoll's blue eyes meet my green eyes. No matter what we are doing. No matter what we are on or if it is how it is. We both have and share the brightest green/orange/silver energy in the reflection of one another's eyes no matter how long I look at her or she looks at me.

This 'SJJ' Mermaid literally came out of the two pictures on my wall immediately after having placed the newest picture the underwater printer just printed out. Shawn's Sat phone got a direct call from Zissafiss and why he is here today.

Shoootzzz braddah! That's why I am here today- Jesus, himself, came down to save me on Hawaii in The Missile Mustang and he introduced me to Babydoll Madison Star.

After the entire event and after seeing the picture of my car. I instantly had a galaxy like vision of Neila's car appear in the air; as if they were one in the same as Amber's eyes appeared to me eight days apart from her death and my birth. This all occurs while Darth is asking about Amber and then Al Capone.

Amber's eyes radiate as Animal Spirits and Spirits combine as the s becomes a z. The color of her eyes form these letters and words below- as they glow:

THE CRYSTAL ROPE

True thoughts expressed with a courage not yet seen
Hoping only for the best from life , why settle for anything less
For others will bring you down if given enough rope
This poem written for you , but I too read the lines between
Enabling myself to untie the knots that have created this whole mess
Your life is more important with it you should cope
For no one is more important ; then you and you alone
This should not be a scary thought for by yourself these knots unwind

Ask for the strength to persevere and in time that too will come

Mostly what is frightening is the not knowing what should be known

This understanding will appear and yourself is no longer in a bind

Seek and it will be answered though you may not know where from

Can anything change other than your perception

Even if it does . . . was it your efforts that finally availed

Would change occur if time had restraints

Honesty with yourself , the roots , of all your questions

If your train of life is dependent upon others , soon it will derail

Is change good if abundant and time is faint

For a faint trace of lipstick upon a crystal glass
will only allow the crystal to glimmer at exactly the right time
Without the correct light , that lipstick makes the crystal obscure
That crystal , your life , should be free of all trespass
The lipstick , seemingly others , eliminate the shine .
The rope - you should pull back and look for your life to endure

After this experience and the experience in the Mustang Missile I felt the need to visit Darth again the next time I was on land.

At the very beginning of the presentation she began to say. "there have been spirits lining up early to attend tonight's Gala like humans line up on Black Friday to get in there favorite stores. . .there is one spirit who decided to cut in front of everyone to make his presence known and direct her to me."

Darth knew of the recent car crash and continues to say, "angels are placed on earth for a number of reasons but one of them is to help save people in need. On very rare occasions- Jesus himself comes down to save people himself but he did in my case because I have something important to do!"

She asked me, "Do you know what the something important thing is?"

I responded, "yes, finish writing my book!" She then added, "the spirits are showing me midget reels from a movie and audio clips of a recording . . . I can hear what they are saying and I recognize a couple of the voices but I can't quite see exactly what they are trying to show me. Part of these midget clips seem to come from a Facebook Reality TV show. There's people you know involved in it and most of them do not like you at all.

One of the midget reels remind me of the Simpsons because it's about the Mustang Missile on Hawaii and it was produced before the accident.

There are spirits all around you and all of them are your guides and protectors. I see at least 15 now but they come and go at will. All of them are showing me this particular midget reel now from the movie entitled 'An Officer and a Gentleman'- symbolic of you in many ways but also as a warning message like 'Halloween Night' the last time you were at this Gala event!"

The spirit which initially cut in front of every other spirit waiting early there interrupts her demandingly, " Tell him to be swift and diligent in making This Point ! The Hell's Kitchen Porn Parody involving his X-Girlfriend and a detective (who may be retired) or says he is retired needs to get out there for people in this world to hear!

The recent Will County Major story just referenced a cabal trying to destroy his life and leave him with nothing sounds quite similar to what has happened here with you but very weak in comparison to what has happened with you. "

Darth asks me , "Do you understand the message so far?"

Shawn responds, " It's Crystal Clear "

The physic named Darth continues, "The spirit lashing out now actually sounds like Kat Williams as he says "This Shit Right Here!"

He is pointing to one of the midget reels involving a $10,000.00 bribe and then finagled rape porn contract using the same dollar amount.

Darth says, "This Officer is Not a Gentleman and I'm referring to Detective Scary who is pretending to be you Shawn and is using your name to better promote himself."

She concludes the spirit guided message by saying, "people know of these midget reels, there are witnesses to the Facebook Reality TV show and there are 2 female witnesses during the running of the water in all of the sinks and showers while 2 males create the twisted video involving one of the infiltrated cattle or sheep.

The landowner is directly involved in the scene with the help of an editor/ writer. One traveled here from another state at the landowner's request to star in the recording based upon the size of his lower extremity.

Everything hidden will become known!"

Many attending the Gala are absolutely startled especially when they learned the Mustang had a recall on the airbag deploying randomly and causing severe eye and head damage. Mine didn't deploy at all! The rug burn like welt in the shape of it formed across my neck. The day before the crash; I was flagged over at one of the check points and given a ticket for not wearing a seatbelt. Normally I didn't.

Many of the locals look at me in amazement saying, "you drove thru cattle country again!"

Some of these landowners are shocked when the initial Police report is filed. So shocked it seems they do not know how to respond. Shoootzzz; there has been no response at all; not to the harassing threat messages left on my office line most likely from "The Officer Who is Not a Gentleman!", not to the Lien Waiver on my largest project in twenty-four years which was used as a headhunting list by the cabal, and not to the recordings /video which they say may not exist because "there was not legal permission to record it!".

Shawn asks during the Will County Video recorded report, "was their legal permission to use my name in a porn parody involving the bribed and or paid ex girlfriend?"

"How about the Facebook Reality TV show involving recognizable voices from my past; was their legal permission to record it? "

Here's the reality and I wish it were a dream. Landowners are creating crime just to create crime while creating crime themselves.

One of the largest and suppressed issues facing this nation is "Human Trafficking"! Paid informants who intentionally create traps for the target of an investigation, mules, cattle, sheep, whom are violated by these landowners are indeed still violated even if they have violated the rights of others in helping the landowners along the way!

A woman's right from a man's perspective is not the point I'm trying to make but it needs to be made. Not to mention the rights of the targeted individual being violated by this same landowner who is most likely the cabal leader behind the creation of the Facebook Reality TV Show and ensuing Hell's Kitchen Porn Parody!

Just a small town; but I don't think it is the girl living in a lonely world! Sounds to me like the landowners have to immediately create a new method of obtaining information without violating the rights of a woman from a gentleman's perspective.

As this book gets passed from another to another and as the audio version gets click after click; I will think of Zissafiss and his clicks and whistle blowing sounds.

The sprouting landowners are similar to the bamboo and are scorched upon impact as this lava flows. The Confucius institutions sprouting up more and more cannot withstand the heat of these truths. As the momentum shifts towards the cabal circle of landowners, the lava is hissing and the salt smelts the skin of the ocean waves upon entry. It is driven through the heart of cattle country landowners!

"Dreamality" is produced within the haze and acidic steam and placed in the Slingshot against THISSSSS part of our world!

To the Hawaiian boyfriend who approached me on the beach expressing concern as to how his X-girlfriend and mother of their child was awarded custody of their child, "with all the drug related police problems and in and out of court to all of a sudden driving around in a nice Range Rover and easily affording a new two-bedroom apartment without a rich boyfriend and without a job"... you were right all along!

Shoootzzz braddah. Mahalo!

CHAPTER XVIII

DEUCES WILD

O-Ee-Yah! Eoh-Ah. O-Ee-Yah! Eoh-Ah. To sound a bit more scary, the landowners are using a low tone to their voices so it comes out quite muffled and honestly, I cannot tell exactly what they are chanting. They are marching back and forth towards one another in what appears to be the front of the Wicked Witch of the West's castle. To me it appears similar to another midget reel from The Simpsons as the moat surrounding the castle starts to fill more and more.

`Their marching steps are slow and deliberate. 1/1, 2/2, 3/3, and 4/4. The rhythmic beat of their steps and chant bring me back to what appears to be reality.

I am in a panic and on the phone with my X-girlfriend who's also in a panic. While looking out my kitchen door towards the backyard, I see the dug trenches created to absorb overflowing water and the sewage lines from the septic field merging together.

"This Shit Right Here!" spoken loudly from Shawn as he looks in amazement to what is occurring around him before taking a deep breath and saying ,"is out of control! This storm moving in on us looks calculated with intent to do harm and serious damage!"

In a manner of minutes listening to the screams and cries out for help- the last two weeks of vacation bliss are like the phone I was just holding in my hand; and are entirely gone!

This particular storm was badgering and sadistically showing little signs of empathy along the way after devastatingly breaking in. Somehow the mini recorder managed to survive what felt like repetitive break ins of my home, body, and mind. The haze lifted around me slowly as my spirit gave way to the other facet controls of my being.

Shawn's eyes are opening wider as continual water flows through the skylight and onto his Bourget Kruzer parked in the living room. There are occasional sparks from wires in the now exposed attic while walking down the hallway. Just before the zag in the zigzag hallway leading to the addition portion of his home, He freezes within his own steps!

The refractions of light seemed to be hitting thousands of crystals along the highlighted path to his feet. A rock within ice is his state. He's expecting to see the letter from Hawaii swoop to the floor from what used to be an eight-foot-tall flat ceiling.

He's seemingly entering what many call a Deja Vu. Shawn likes to refer to them as checkpoints from God when they occur. He's dizzy and beginning to seize slightly as a large crystal tube chamber appears on the floor going through the ground and into the underworld while connecting to the sky at the same exact time.

Leading to the master bedroom are repetitive glass floors; all with higher hierarchy within the 45-degree ceiling . It seems he is able to walk again but the floating plains of glass smoothly transition him from one panel to the next.

Between these sensations occurring within Shawn and around Shawn, he's standing in awe. The 45-degree ceiling leads to no ceiling at all and to the highest wall of his home which is no longer there. The sky's the limit easily defined by the different levels of glass floating floors between himself. It's as if the roof is one of the Hulk's Tshirts being ripped off and he's just as scared seeing and hearing it as well.

In front of Shawn, where the 42' long massive straight wall used to stand, is now an arch shaped wall of glass equally as long and equally as high. The ends of it are bending towards him as they curve even more holding back the water. Although beautiful; it's like nothing he has seen at the Shedd Aquarium because it is equally as scary. Water begins flowing from the soffits of the second floor level. What used to be his Nemo stuffed animal hanging on my bathroom wall above the double doors begins effortlessly floating through different channels of tiles above his fireplace and into the Thomas Kinkade shower curtain which is at the highest part of what's left to the ceiling.

The more and more apparent tapping of the huge cracking water wall of glass in front of Shawn- the more he is rhythmically reminded of his office phone and Woodpecker.

For two days in a row the tapping had been the most consistent, encouraging him to look into the meaning of them both just yesterday!

According to the book entitled "Animal Spirits Guide", written by Stephen D. Farmer, PH.D., this woodpecker was right on point: "A storm is brewing, either literally or metaphorically; but have faith as you're protected no matter what!"

According to the AT&T repairman he had, "not ever seen anything before like it because your office line was crossed into a module with five other lines!" Shawn replies, "does it in anyway explain how the thermostat started playing songs thru it for the first time?"

AT&T repairman states, "maybe it does, since you did not have Wi-Fi turned on your phone . . . it is very possible someone's phone may have connected to it intentionally or unintentionally. They would need your password though!"

Hearing him say this shortly after reading the intrepid message from the woodpecker began a fast forward trip in reverse and into the future it seems . . . as the crackling noises all around him become a silent pause.

The silent pause of the second feels like a minute, the minute feels like a day and the day feels like years as the dream reality world merges with a nightmare. Within the timeframe of whatever this may be- Shawn sees visual viewers below paying a membership fee to see.

There was a power and control battle occurring represented by arrows bordering the circle which sometimes aligned themselves in direct opposites of one another. Other times they flowed the same way creating a whirlpool like effect underneath Shawn. They must have stayed in opposition with one another for far too long for this to happen as the sound of the tempered glass tapping became a repetitive golf ball dinging sound off metal, plastic and glass combined. Louder and louder with more and more consistency.

"I'm chill babe, yes I'm the chillest. Gonna swarm stage, gonna kill this!" are lyrics of the song playing in the background; part of a song he has not yet finished writing. It's a song he has not ever performed before and before going backstage.

In response to Shawn asking one of his friends how she was doing he hears, "my mouthpiece is still working; so doing as good as can be out here in Milwaukee."

After hearing this he laughs while picturing his X-fiancé's car getting stolen from the garage well before she is photographed hugging up on Joe Biden from the back.

He sees the front and back of a postcard he designed while attending The University of Florida. It is addressed to Donald Trump at Trump Headquarters from someone who cares with his old Gainesville Florida return address. The postcard's meaning explained on the back saying , "try turning the postcard over (rotate the center - your center) and the world will come into focus."

At that exact moment within the ever paused occurring second in his life there was peace and harmony. He is back in Gainesville staring at a painting on the wall as these words flow thru:

I didn't know life without you
that same life I wanted to forget
when I was twenty-two.
Couldn't begin to understand
we were on the rocks together
and you held my hand
more tightly than any person can
much stronger; as I became a man
I couldn't let go no matter how hard I tried
I saw my reflection as I began to cry
in the bottom of the glass as I began to ask God why. . .
Then I realized that my life had just begun
when I saw my reflection.

Staring at the painting on the wall
how the canvass seems to soften
when the man losses it all
Abruptly falling to his knees
the sand begins to scatter; his thoughts
framing his apologies
more tightly than any person can
much stronger; as I became a man
I couldn't let go no matter how hard I tried
I saw my reflection as I began to cry
in the painting of the man
as he began to ask, "God why?"
Then I realized that my life had just begun
when I saw my reflection.

It was as if the floodgates were about to break open as darkness took over the land. It was about noon when the earthquake coincided with the crucifixion as Jesus cried out again in a loud voice, "Eloi, Eloi, lema sabachthani?" (which means "My God, My God; why have you forsaken me?")... giving up his spirit in his breath.

Similar yet different to the slang term "Haole" being muttered by one of the Hawaiian uncles expressing his discontent of the police department, "they are acting as if their King Kong exploiting our wahine and using them against our kane!"

At that moment the curtain of the temple was torn in two from top to bottom. The earth shook, the rocks split, and the tombs broke open.

"Gatehouses mistaken for the mansion cause as many issues as the intended design of the gatehouses themselves." said in the background and then repeated by two of the aunties attending the meeting.

Shawn finally starts coming to while laying on the concrete slab of his house floor and appears to be in reality but unsure if it's present day. He says, "Good Lord!" to the reflection in the puddle beneath himself when he sees each of his body parts represented with different petals yet all of the same Chandramallika flower. Meaning: "Queen who resides on the Moon."

In between the reflection of his real (eyes) and eyes- there is a crystal chamber keeping them entranced; similar to the one Shawn saw earlier in the hallway connecting the underworld and the heavens but much smaller. It begins buzzing, dimming and flickering until there is no light at all. The reflection in the puddle disappears the instant the crystal chamber disappears.

Shawn aimlessly looks around for a bit and walks towards what used to be the outer wall of his home. His garage is gone and so is the fence on that side of the yard.

Beyond the fence used to be his neighbor's house, a street, and a row of houses on both sides of the street. They are all gone and replaced with a golf course.

"Ahhh" Shawn says, "This helps explain the repetitive golf balls hitting the house in the wee hours of the morning!" A golf cart comes rolling up and one of the men yells out, "Sure glad you're okay Mr. Bosi. Wish I could say the same for your home. In a way it was probably good you weren't home when this happened!"

Shawn replies, "Thanks. I guess that's what insurance is for. By the way, I was home while it happened!"

The men are now standing outside of the golf cart and begin looking around with me at all the destruction caused around me. All of us shaking our heads in amazement.

The roof in the bible represents what is inmost in a person--the part that is closest and most in contact with the Lord. The roof lifted off also means more people knowing of my current situation right now.

The tornado is a destructive outside force spinning out of control similar to the created storm in my life; fabricated and created while directly tampering with my personal, business, and social life.

Both the roof and tornado have significant meaning to me at this particular time in my life. An informant not obtaining enough information on me getting raped in the fifth year of our relationship. Another one making an out of the blue phone call ended with, "the world doesn't need any more whistleblowers right now!"

Some ranchers who I have known for quite some time sever all ties and communication. Shoootz, my own business associates disappear without any communication or response to calls and texts. My X-girlfriend obviously placed in their same category after categorically denying the FB Reality TV and ensuing Hell's Kitchen Porno Parody.

The phrase "If you can't stand the heat- get out of the kitchen!" takes on an entirely new meaning while hearing the morbid excerpts playing from the mini recorder before, during and after the editing process which takes place within the same hour by the same people in the privacy of her home.

Her terrifying screams and calls out for help are muffled by the television playing loudly along with the running of water in all three sinks, the shower, and the tub. The large extremities forced down her throat also included jalapeño peppers in between was ungodly and sadistic to say the least.

There are two females present guarding the front and back door while this occurs; one of them referenced as Amanda during the preparation of the onslaught. The preparation took place while they gained illegal access into my X-girlfriends home to set up the proper cameras and microphones. "Hi Amanda- I see we have a new group working together for the first time today!", says Detective Scary (who's not a gentleman) as bags are opened noticeably after the doorbell rings.

There are discussions both inside the illegally entered home and also inside what appears to be the editing van or home in close proximity to the planned onslaught. Their communications heard plainly as they mix and edit part of the actual cooking program which is recorded and next in line to be watched by my X-girlfriend. Obvious on many occasions such as , " Wow, that was hard to fit all of it in there but that sounds great !', said excitedly by Detective Scary.

There's a lot of back-and-forth communication between the person who traveled from another state to play the lead role and this scary, so-called detective/ officer who is not a gentleman, plainly heard after they initially left the premises.

They can hear myself and my ex girlfriend arguing over the phone as one of them comments, " I really like how all of this is coming together. The plan itself has worked perfectly and now that they are fighting it makes it even better !"

Their back-and-forth communication continues with, " ...Shawn Bosi- he is a very smart guy; well intelligent. He likes to talk dirty. He could do so much better than her but fell for 'the babe in the woods' routine."

Meanwhile, the screen door in the back of the house seems to be opening and closing with unfamiliar voices every 15-20 minutes it seems.

One voice questions upon entry, "Do you live alone or is there anyone else here?" Shortly after an inaudible quiet response, the sound of a woman going down on a man is very obvious. It's a fairly quick occurrence followed by an even quicker "thank you!" said.

The sound of the patio door opening and apparently closing yet again is interrupted by the sound of a very loud burp as the officer who is not a gentleman says, "what a pig!" in response.

During the entire time of the monitored informant's house, with the door opening and closing, Detective Scary continues to count down:

"Forty-Five minutes till go time!"

Followed by, "Thirty minutes till go time !"

I hear one half of a phone call taken in between these events and I real (eyes) she is answering a call from me. It's the night before my colonoscopy and I have already started to drink the gallon of fluid. I'm familiar with the conversation based upon what I hear her saying to me.

The two male voices begin to chat in the background as Detective Scary says, "Problem is Shawn is a tough guy and may actually come here during the production. He might have a heart attack if he walks in seeing this. Maybe he will be scared though and want to have a couple beers and just watch!"

The out of state traveler makes himself known by saying in response, "I know he was just on a two-week vacation with her but we have a very limited timeframe to get this recording done and I traveled here . . . so he's not fucking this up! If we have to brown bag him we will. If he comes here- I will destroy him!"

The name of the state he traveled from is said clearly in the recording along with so many other incriminating details. Those and other written down details along with my hard drive are later stolen while celebrating my 50'th B-day with "SSJ' Mermaid in California less than three months later.

I did not need those written down details to place this in writing. Nor did I need to listen to the onslaught again.

"FIFTEEN MINUTES till go Time!"

At about that time I real (eyes) what is occurring. It seems as if the sexual acts being performed are being monitored as the countdown to the bust and ensuing production is going to occur.

By then it is too late as it has already happened. The pieces of the puzzle quickly and decisively start to put themselves together but the tragedy and the aftermath already heard and experienced has already been explained but in reverse.

The realization of the dream and reality experiences become more of a consistent nightmare the more and more the recordings are rewound and listened to. It seems as if these odd occurrences become even more odd than already explained as Shawn's name is heard in the background with a very strange repetitive chant during the actual onslaught itself . . . " Oh, oh, oh, oh, Shaaawwn Bosssiii. Oh, oh, oh, oh, Shaaawwn Bosssiii !"

I decide to stop listening to the horrificness of this recording right after I hear one of the two female landowners guarding one of the entrances say, "I have seen enough! Is this what we do now to women who like sucking cock? I like sucking cock and this is not what I signed up for. I am out of here!"

My heart drops more as my stomach smashes it!

"Dreamality" is produced within the haze and acidic steam. It's placed in the Slingshot against THISSSSS part of our world!

THISSSS part of the world is seemingly creating and editing more and more. Creating experiences in my life in pursuit of creating a reaction which would place me behind bars. To destroy my freedoms while slowly replacing them with freedumbs.

Why again are most people in THISSSS world considered "Have Nots!" ? Banks Have Not!

Government's Have Not!

In some cases, family, and friends Have Not!

Enemies Have Not!

I know it's not only me having these thoughts. It's many of us haves and haves nots. At least half of our halves have knots. It's virtually impossible, with or without God, seemingly not to have knots and unfortunately our holograms cannot mimic ourselves and the Meta World's view is seemingly part of THISSSS.

"Those with ears shall hear. Those with eyes shall see."

By this time Shawn thought he had heard and seen enough. He was certain to have developed a PTSD from just hearing the experience nonetheless living through them.

The day he heard edited recordings being placed in other staged and circumvented recorded events which were already multiple crimes being created by people whom said oaths under God to protect and serve others from crime- he knew all of this was happening for a reason. Jesus was the reason. He is and he was. He did and He does protect and serve his children. There are no odds big enough to stack against his works and the protection of his angels' works.

Even a detective wanting to be Shawn Bosi can't be the real Shawn Bosi who owns Upright Fences Downright Decks and Patios Inc.

Eminem would say, " Will the Real Shawn Bosi ' Please Stand Up ' !

Well, he did and he does.

The police department owning the "IMDB" label is just as bad as any police department in the U.S. being owned by The Republic of China.

Trump stopped The Chicago Board of Trade going into Chinese hands years ago. How exactly are our police departments in the U.S. any different?

Recordings of a crime being committed to create crime being edited and audited to stage an event to place a local business owner behind bars who has not created a crime seems a bit Confucius to me. Shawn, like Eminem, knows what peeps will say and have said to him and about him:

1) " You're just a small-town boy who's born and raised in the same small town!

2) How are you any different than other local business owners?

3) Why will others want to read your book anyways?

4) Are you sure you want to go down that rabbit hole?

5) You're facing a giant because some of these jealous locals run this same town and some of them have authority! "

6) The former Mayor filed a Federal lawsuit against former Joliet Police Chief and The City of Joliet in Will County.

To these he will politely respond with:

1) " I graduated from H. S. early and have been self-reliant since an early age.

2) Uhhhm... we are all different in our own ways but my winter's on Hawaii while owning my company along with my outlook on life certainly separates me from most.

3) It's written to help redesign the matrix of the world we are living in. Although it is about my story ...it is not branded in that fashion!

4) I was already dragged much further down after going into it. I was pulled from the underground and flooded rabbit hole which was spiraling out of control like an EF-5 Tornado by Zissafiss. The 'SSJ' Mermaid spun like Lucinda Ruh as those flood waters froze over more and more to the point of forming a crystallized water sprite of every color describe earlier before.

5) I love the movie 'Facing The Giants'. God makes a Way out of No Way! These locals in this town might be deemed Giants to some but there's a much bigger Goliath in the room and it's not an elephant. It's not King Kong either.

Eminem's rap named "White America" was like a "Nan Nan Nan"; as if he was Jackson L. Fox rapping to Black America.

When there's a point to be made which impacts all races in every nation on earth; sometimes you just have to make it.

If you're like me and support the Raider Nation, you will know the story of Easy-E and Ice Cube. Their West Coast gangster rap helped propel NWA during the time of Rodney King. They had funky ass bass lines with hard lyrics about real topics!

This book obviously has a funky ass bass line with hard lyrics about real topics; thus, the two fingers broke in the process of typing it.

Whether I'm white and country saying, "I still got er done!" or whether I'm black and southern saying, " I got it did!"- those are semantics to me.

What's not semantics to me is the silence of a sitting president during an election while silencing other government officials and entertainers etc. by Twitter and Facebook!

No matter what color of skin we have, those should not be semantics for any of us. As people of the world, I believe we have seen and heard enough.

The emphasis of strategic thinking in organizations is not better than getting things done more quickly especially if crimes are created in the process. Seems like a slow march through institutions to me.

The steps are slow and deliberate. 1/1, 2/2, 3/3, and 4/4.

What first appeared to be overlapping voices of American and Japanese; were American and Chinese! As the s becomes a z.